Oh What a Lovely War

Oh What a Lovely War was born on the stage of the Theatre Royal, Stratford. The scheme for a chronicle of the First World War, told through the songs and documents of the period, was given flesh and blood in Joan Littlewood's Theatre Workshop, where every production, and this one *par excellence*, was the fruit of close co-operation between writer, actor and director. The whole team participated in detailed research into the period and in the creative task of bringing their material to life in theatrical terms.

The result was an entertainment which won the acclaim of London audiences and critics and the *Grand Prix* of the *Théâtre des Nations* festival in Paris in 1963 and has become a classic of the modern theatre. In 1969 the film version became a popular success in its own right.

OH WHAT A
LOVELY WAR

BY

Theatre Workshop
Charles Chilton
and the members of the
original cast

Military adviser:
RAYMOND FLETCHER

LONDON
METHUEN & CO LTD
11 NEW FETTER LANE EC4

This play is fully protected by copyright. All inquiries concerning performing rights, professional or amateur, should be directed to Theatre Workshop, Theatre Royal, Stratford, London E15.

NOTE TO THE READER

This is a play script and should be read as such.

ACKNOWLEDGEMENTS

Lines from the songs, 'Belgium put the Kibosh on the Kaiser', 'Hold Your Hand Out, Naughty Boy', 'I'll Make a Man of You', 'Goodbye-ee', 'Sister Susie's Sewing Shirts', 'Pack Up Your Troubles', 'Row, Row, Row,', and 'Hitchy-Koo' are reprinted by permission of the copyright owners and publishers, Francis Day & Hunter Ltd; the copyright owners in Australasia ('Belgium put the Kibosh on the Kaiser', 'Hold Your Hand Out, Naughty Boy', 'I'll Make a Man of You', 'Goodbye-ee', 'Sister Susie's Sewing Shirts', 'Pack Up Your Troubles'), Messrs. J. Albert & Son Pty. Ltd; the copyright owners in Canada ('Pack Up Your Troubles'), Chappell & Co. Inc., New York; the copyright owners in Canada and Australasia ('Row, Row, Row,'), H. von Tilzer Music Publishing Co; and the copyright owners in Canada and Australasia ('Hitchy-Koo'), La Salle Music Publishers, Inc. 'Keep the Home Fires Burning': copyright © 1915 by Ascherberg, Hopwood & Crew Ltd; copyright renewed; reprinted by permission of Ascherberg, Hopwood & Crew Ltd, London, and Chappell & Co. Inc., New York. 'I Wore a Tunic' is a soldiers' parody of the song 'I wore a Tulip', published by Ascherberg, Hopwood & Crew Ltd, London and Leo Feist Inc., New York. Lines from the song, 'Are We Downhearted' are reproduced by permission of Lawrence Wright Music Co. Ltd. Lines from the songs, 'Oh! It's a Lovely War', 'There's a Long, Long Trail', 'It's a Long, Long Way to Tipperary' and the soldiers' parody 'Hush, here comes a Whizzbang' ('Hush, here comes the Dream Man') are reproduced by permission of B. Feldman & Co. Ltd.

First published in 1965
paperback edition 1967
Reprinted 1969 and 1971
© *1965 by Joan Littlewood Productions Ltd*
Printed in Great Britain by
W. & J. Mackay & Co Ltd, Chatham
S.B.N. 416 19400 1 (paperback edition)
S.B.N. 416 65090 2 (hardbound edition)

OH WHAT A LOVELY WAR was first presented by Theatre Workshop at the Theatre Royal, Stratford, London E15, on 19th March 1963, with the following cast:

THE PIERROTS

Ann Beach	Griffith Davies
Fanny Carby	John Gower
Bettina Dickson	Colin Kemball
Myvanwy Jenn	Murray Melvin
	Brian Murphy
Barry Bethell	George Sewell
Brian Cronin	Victor Spinetti
Larry Dann	Bob Stevenson

The play was subsequently presented at the Wyndham's Theatre, London (first performance 20th June 1963) with the following cast:

Avis Bunnage	John Gower
Fanny Carby	Tony Holland
Judy Cornwell	Godfrey James
Myvanwy Jenn	Colin Kemball
Mary Preston	Murray Melvin
	Brian Murphy
Barry Bethell	Joseph Powell
Larry Dann	George Sewell
Griffith Davies	Victor Spinetti
George Giles	Bob Stevenson

A THEATRE WORKSHOP GROUP PRODUCTION
under the direction of
JOAN LITTLEWOOD

Setting by John Bury
Choreography by Bob Stevenson
Costumes by Una Collins

The photographs show scenes from the original production.
Photographs: Romano Cagnoni (Report)
The drawings are by Una Collins.

Act One

OVERTURE

LONG LONG TRAIL.
LAND OF HOPE AND GLORY.
OH IT'S A LOVELY WAR.
MADEMOISELLE FROM ARMENTIÈRES.
GOODBYE-EE.
LINE OF LAND OF HOPE AND GLORY.
LONG LONG TRAIL.
PACK UP YOUR TROUBLES.
LINE OF NATIONAL ANTHEM.
I DO LIKE TO BE BESIDE THE SEASIDE.

The stage is set as for a pierrot show of fifty years ago with red, white, and blue fairy lights, twin balconies left and right and coloured circus 'tubs', which are used as seats, etc., throughout the play. Above the stage there is a Newspanel across which messages are flashed during the action. There is also a screen behind the acting area, on to which slides are projected.

The pierrots enter during the end of the overture and watch the newspanel. The Master of Ceremonies, one of the pierrots, wears a mortar board.

NEWSPANEL: SUMMER 1914. SCORCHING BANK HOLIDAY FORECAST . . . GUNBOAT SMITH FOULS CARPENTIER IN SIXTH ROUND . . . OPERA BLOSSOMS UNDER THOMAS BEECHAM.

M.C. Everybody in? Come along, madam; we're just starting. What'll we do?
PIERROT. How about 'Johnny Jones'?

M.C. O.K. Jones it is.

As the intro to 'Row, Row, Row' starts the pierrots run to their positions and sing:

SONG.   ROW, ROW, ROW

> Young Johnny Jones he had a cute little boat
> And all the girlies he would take for a float.
> He had girlies on the shore,
> Sweet little peaches, by the score –
> But master Johnny was a wise 'un, you know,
> His steady girl was Flo
> And every Sunday afternoon
> She'd jump in his boat
> And they would spoon.

CHORUS. And then he'd row, row, row,
> Way up the river he would row, row, row,
> A hug he'd give her
> Then he'd kiss her now and then,
> She would tell him when,
> They'd fool around and fool around
> And then they'd kiss again.
> And then he'd row, row, row,
> A little further he would go, oh, oh, oh,
> Then he'd drop both his oars,
> Take a few more encores,
> And then he'd row, row, row.

(*Repeat the chorus until . . .*)

> A little further he would go, oh, oh, oh,
> Then we'll drop both our oars,
> Take a round of applause,
> And then we'll go, go, go.

M.C. Off and change! (*All except the M.C. go off. The M.C. picks up a ringmaster's whip.*) Good evening, all: seat for you

Row, row, row

here, darling. Any more? Right; close the doors. Welcome
to our little pierrot show; 'The Merry Roosters'. You've just
witnessed our opening number. We've got songs for you, a
few battles and some jokes. I've got the whip to crack in case
you don't laugh. (*To the pierrots.*) Are you ready?

PIERROTS. No!

M.C. Good. Time for a joke. Did you hear the one about the
German Admiral Graf Von and his three daughters, Knit
Von, Pearl Von, and Plain Von. You should have laughed
at that; it was the best gag in the show. [*Or:* I'm glad you
laughed at that 'cos it's the worst gag in the show.] Shall I
tell you another one? There were these two Generals went
paddling, you see; they were down at Frinton and in the
water, when one General looked at the other General and
said, 'Good God, Reggie, your feet are filthy!' 'Damn it all,
man,' said the other General, 'I wasn't here last year . . .'
You see he couldn't get the soap . . . Oh, never mind. You
ready now?

PIERROTS. .Yes!

M.C. Good. Milords, ladies and gentlemen, may we perform
for you the ever-popular War Game!

BAND.   MARCH OF THE GLADIATORS

*Circus Parade: two pierrot-acrobats lead on the company
dressed in national costumes. A French group of three pierrots –
one man (a French army officer), two women; a German group –
the Kaiser and a woman, Austria; a British group of five – a
woman, Ireland, leading, a British colonial on the shoulders of
another, followed by a fan-holder, and a coloured servant;
Russian group of two men. The company move round the stage
in a circle as in a circus parade, finally stopping, keeping the
circular shape, when the German group is downstage centre on
the second time round.*

NEWSPANEL. TROOPS FIRE ON DUBLIN CROWD – AUG I

BRITISH CABINET VOTE AGAINST HELPING FRANCE IF
WAR COMES – LIBERALS VOTE FOR NEUTRALITY UNDER
ANY CIRCUMSTANCES – GERMANY SENDS 40,000 RIFLES
TO ULSTER.

M.C. (*as the nations pass*). La Belle France – Upright, steadfast
Germany – Good morning, sir – The first part of the game is
called 'Find the Thief'.

BAND.   SONS OF THE SEA

BRITAIN. Look here, we own 30 million square miles of colo-
nies. The British Empire is the most magnificent example of
working democracy the world has ever seen.

VOICE. Hear absolutely hear.

M.C. And the lady on my right.

BAND.   SI LE VIN EST BON

FRENCHWOMAN. La République.

FRENCHMAN. The seat of reason, the centre of world civilization – culture, and l'amour.

M.C. They're at it again. Stop it. If they're not doing that,
they're eating. How big's your acreage.

FRENCHWOMAN. Six million square kilometres.

M.C. And you ?

BAND.   GERMAN MUSIC

KAISER. Germany – a mere three million square kilometres.
But we are a new nation united only since 1871.

FRENCHMAN. When you stole Alsace-Lorraine.

KAISER. Ours, German.

M.C. Hey, we haven't started to play the game yet.

KAISER. We are a disciplined, moral, industrious people. We
want more say in the world's affairs.

M.C. Have to keep an eye on you . . . (*To the band.*) Let's
have the Russian Anthem.

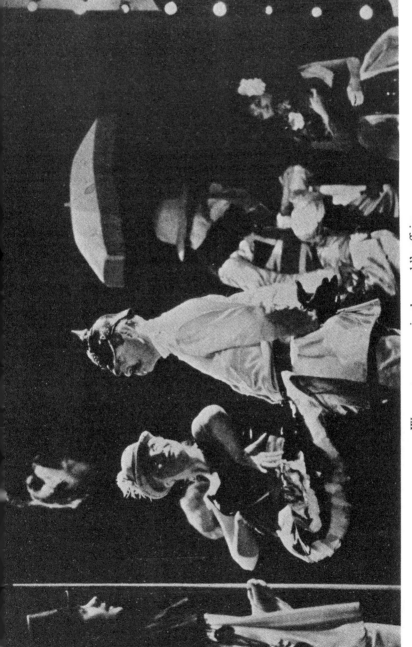

We want more say in the world's affairs

You're in the three-mile limit. You're all right.

BAND.   RUSSIAN ANTHEM

RUSSIA. They're all Yids.

NEWSPANEL. CHURCHILL ORDERS FLEET TO SCAPA FLOW.

M.C. (*to audience*). The second part of the War Game. The Plans.

BAND.   GERMAN MUSIC

KAISER. War is unthinkable. It is out of the question.

FRENCHMAN. It would upset the balance of power.

BRITAIN. It would mean the ruin of the world, undoubtedly.

FRENCHMAN. Besides, our alliances make us secure.

KAISER. But if you threaten us, then we have the supreme deterrent, which we will not hesitate to use . . .

M.C. Ssh . . . secret.

The M.C. whistles. The stage darkens and the screen comes down. Everyone leaves but the Kaiser and Austria. General Moltke enters. Russia, France, and Britain listen at the doors.

Slide 1: Map showing the Schlieffen plan of 1914 for an attack on Paris.

MOLTKE. The German Army will win this battle by an envelopment with the right wing, and let the last man brush the Channel with his sleeve.

KAISER. Violate the neutrality of Belgium and the Netherlands?

MOLTKE. World power or downfall. Liège twelve days after mobilization M. Day, Brussels M.19, French frontier M.22, and we will enter Paris at 11.30 on the morning of M.39. I send all the best brains in the War College into the Railway Section.

KAISER. And the Russians?

MOLTKE. They won't be ready till 1916.

M.C. (*whistles*). Time's up.

BAND.   SI LE VIN EST BON

Slide 2: Map showing the French 'Plan 17' of 1914 for a French offensive.

FRENCHMAN. France admits no law but the offensive. Advance with all forces to attack the German Army. France, her bugles sounding, her soldiers armed for glory, her will to conquer. An idea and a sword. Besides, they will attack Russia first.

Slide 3: Russian infantry marching with rifles.

RUSSIA. The Russian steam roller. We have a million and a half bayonets. Better than bullets any day. Once in motion, we go rolling forward inex –

M.C. Inexorably. Hey, the bar's open, go and have a quick drink. – Hey, you've got snow on your boots!

M.C. blows bo'suns' pipe.

Slide 4: A British battleship berthed at a pier.

BAND.   LAND OF HOPE AND GLORY

BRITISH ADMIRAL. Well done. In the event of a war, the Royal Navy will keep more than a million Germans busy. We shall disembark on a ten-mile strip of hard sand on the northern shores of Prussia and draw off more than our weight of numbers from the fighting line. The overwhelming supremacy of the British Navy is the only thing to keep the Germans out of Paris.

M.C. Hear, hear.

BRITISH GENERAL. On a point of order, sir, your plans appear to have little in common with those of the Army.

BRITISH ADMIRAL. Look here, you soldiers are a pretty grotesque lot with your absurd ideas about war. Happily you are powerless. We could go right ahead and leave you to go fooling around the Vosges. Have you got a plan?

BRITISH GENERAL. Of course.

Slide 5: A blank.

BRITISH ADMIRAL. Yes, I thought so.

The Company intone the words: 'Peace in our time O Lord.' M.C. blows whistle.

M.C. Any questions so far? Got all the plans off? Good. (*To the band.*) Let's have the schmalzy bit. 'Find the Anarchist'. I can't help you any more, because I play a statue in this.

NEWSPANEL. SARAJEVO.

BAND.   SMETANA: RICHARD III

Promenade: the company enter and perform a dance-cum-Sunday afternoon promenade as in the town of Sarajevo: army officers paying court to the ladies, the junior ones being continually ousted by more senior ones, etc. The scene is ended by a pistol shot. Sounds of rain and thunder. As the shot is fired the stage empties and a street vendor wheels on a beer stall, on which hangs a small portrait of the Archduke Ferdinand. Two drinkers, secret policemen in plain clothes, talk at the stall.

SERBIAN SECRET POLICEMAN. Ein dunkeles Bier, bitte.

AUSTRO-HUNGARIAN SECRET POLICEMAN. Did you hear that?

SERBIAN. You mean that shot?

AUSTRO-HUNGARIAN. Ja.

SERBIAN. No, I heard nothing.

AUSTRO-HUNGARIAN. I'll have a Bier, please.

SERBIAN. Lovely weather we're having.

AUSTRO HUNGARIAN. Ja, ja, very good.

SERBIAN You say somebody shot somebody?

It was either a Catholic, a Protestant, a Jew or a Serb or a Croat . . .

AUSTRO-HUNGARIAN. Ja, ja, the Archduke Ferdinand, the big one.

SERBIAN. No.

AUSTRO-HUNGARIAN. Ja.

SERBIAN. Who did he shoot?

AUSTRO-HUNGARIAN. No, he was shot.

SERBIAN. Do they know who did it?

AUSTRO-HUNGARIAN. That is the question.

The stallholder takes down the picture of the Archduke.

He was driving in a motor car.

SERBIAN. Very dangerous things, motor cars.

AUSTRO-HUNGARIAN. With the Archduchess.

SERBIAN. Big fat Sophie.

The Austro-Hungarian starts taking notes.

AUSTRO-HUNGARIAN. Ja, big fat Sophie. With a revolver.

SERBIAN. Should have used a pistol. A Browning automatic. With a Browning automatic can you shoot ten archdukes and ten archduchesses.

AUSTRO-HUNGARIAN. Do you know who did it?

(*To stallholder.*) Do you know who did it?

STALLHOLDER. No. I never meddle in politics.

AUSTRO-HUNGARIAN. Then what have you done with the Archduke Ferdinand's portrait?

STALLHOLDER. I had to take it down. The flies have done their business on it.

SERBIAN. I will tell you exactly who did it.

AUSTRO-HUNGARIAN. Yes?

SERBIAN. It was either a Catholic, a Protestant, a Jew, or a Serb, or a Croat, or a young Czech Liberal, or an Anarchist, or a Syndicalist. In any case it means war.

AUSTRO-HUNGARIAN. You think so?

SERBIAN. Of course. 'Bang', says Austria, 'shoot my nephew,

would you? There's one in the schmackers for you.' Then
in comes Kaiser Willie to help Austria, in comes Russia to
help Serbia, and in comes France because they hated Germany since 1871.

AUSTRO-HUNGARIAN (*writing on a pad*). '. . . . because they
hated Germany since 1871.' Very good, thank you. Would
you sign this please?

SERBIAN (*signing*). This war has been coming for a long time.

AUSTRO-HUNGARIAN. Ja, I am glad you think so. Step out on
to the pavement. I am a member of the Austro-Hungarian
Secret Police.

SERBIAN. And I am a member of the Serbian Secret Police.

AUSTRO-HUNGARIAN. Ah! We liquidated you yesterday – I
arrest you for high treason.

SERBIAN. What about him?

AUSTRO-HUNGARIAN. Good idea. We arrest you.

STALLHOLDER. But I've said nothing!

AUSTRO-HUNGARIAN. You said the flies could scheister on the
Kaiser. Left, right, left, right . . . (*As they move off.*)

SERBIAN. This means war.

BAND.   TWELFTH STREET RAG

All three go off. Two newsboys run across the stage.

FIRST NEWSBOY. Special! Austria declares war on Serbia!

SECOND NEWSBOY. Extra! Russia mobilizes! Russia mobilizes!

Two girls cross the stage pushing a tandem bicycle.

FIRST GIRL. Russia mobilizes?

SECOND GIRL. Ja, and Papa says France must stand by Russia.

FIRST GIRL. Oh! Is that good?

*Two German businessmen pass with bowler hats and dispatch-
cases.*

FIRST BUSINESSMAN. I understand that we have ordered

Russia to demobilize within twelve hours. The point is will France remain neutral?

SECOND BUSINESSMAN. Russia is asking for time.

FIRST BUSINESSMAN. Where did you hear that?

SECOND BUSINESSMAN. It's all over town.

FIRST BUSINESSMAN. War's off, then?

SECOND BUSINESSMAN. Yes. War is off.

FIRST BUSINESSMAN. Good. Otto, Otto, the war is off.

A female ballet dancer enters dancing to ballet music.

CROWD (*offstage*). Good! Good! Hurrah!

DANCER (*to audience*). Damen und Herren, the German ultimatum to Russia has expired.

A bell rings. All those who made entrances in the last scene retrace their steps and take up positions onstage, for the reading of the Declaration of Mobilization.

GERMAN HERALD (*on a balcony at the side of the stage*). Ich bestimme hiermit, das Deutsche Heer und die Kaiserliche Marine, sind nach Massgabe des Mobilmachungsplans für das Deutsche Heer und die Kaiserliche Marine kriegsbereit aufzustellen. Der Zweite August 1914 wird als erster Mobilmachungstag festgesetzt. Berlin Ersten August 1914. Wilhelm König von Preussen und Deutscher Kaiser. Bethman Hollweg (Reichskanzler).

FEMALE STATION ANNOUNCER. All civilian trains cancelled.

MALE STATION ANNOUNCER. All civilian trains cancelled.

FEMALE STATION ANNOUNCER. Until further notice, there will be no more passenger trains leaving this station.

MALE STATION ANNOUNCER. Until further notice, there will be no more passenger trains leaving this station.

The Kaiser enters with Moltke.

KAISER. The world will be engulfed in the most terrible of wars, the ultimate aim of which is the ruin of Germany.

England, France and Russia have conspired together for our annihilation.

MOLTKE. France has mobilized. Your Majesty.

KAISER. The encirclement of Germany is an accomplished fact. We have run our heads into a noose. England?

MOLTKE. They have not yet made up their minds.

KAISER. Abandon the Plan.

MOLTKE. It is too late. The wheels are already in motion.

KAISER. Send a telegram to my cousin George V, notifying him my troops are being prevented by telephone and telegram from passing through Belgium.

Two soldiers with field telephones run on and sit at opposite sides of the stage. Sound of morse tapping.

FRENCHMAN. War might burst from a clump of trees – a meeting of two patrols – a threatening gesture – a black look – a brutal word – a shot.

ENGLISHMAN. The lamps are going out all over Europe. We shall not see them lit again in our lifetime.

ENGLISH SOLDIER. 'Ere – they've gone into Luxembourg.

LUXEMBOURG SOLDIER. Notify England, France, Belgium, a platoon of Germans has gone into Luxembourg.

KAISER. Notify Lieutenant Feldmann that he is to withdraw immediately from Luxembourg.

ENGLISH SOLDIER. No, it is a mistake.

MOLTKE. Advance into Luxembourg.

KAISER. Advance.

LUXEMBOURG SOLDIER. Platoon withdrawn.

ENGLISH SOLDIER. They've gone in all right . . . eh? . . . Blimey! We're off! They've crossed into Belgium an' all!

Explosion. The lights go out. Full stage lighting flashes on. The whole company is standing in a semicircle grinning and clapping wildly but soundlessly. The band plays a line of the National Anthem. All the pierrots stand to attention.

M.C. Will the lady in the second row kindly remove that dachshund.

The pierrots move to go off. The band plays a line of 'The Marseillaise'. They move to go off again. The band plays a line of the Belgian Anthem (two-thirds through). Nobody knows it. They turn to watch the newspanel.

NEWSPANEL. AUG 4 BRITAIN DECLARES WAR ON GERMANY.

The M.C. blows a whistle. The screen comes down.

M.C. Well, that's the end of Part One of the War Game.

The band plays a chorus of 'We don't want to lose you', during which the pierrots go off one by one, as slides of the coming of war in different countries are shown, ending up with the Kitchener poster.

Slide sequence:
Slide 5: British civilian volunteers, marching in column of fours from recruiting office.
Slide 6: Street parade of civilians led by young boys, one with Union Jack and another playing the bagpipes.
Slide 7: Crowd of German civilians cheering a military parade.
Slide 8: Another parade of British civilians being led by young boys, one with Union Jack, another playing a drum.
Slide 9: Young British girls dancing in the streets.
Slide 10: Crowd of British volunteers outside a recruiting office.
Slide 11: Eton schoolboys marching with rifles at the slope.
Slide 12: Poster of Kitchener pointing, with caption 'Your Country Needs You'.

The girls sing a verse and chorus of 'We don't want to lose you'.

The band plays a half-chorus of the song. Mime tableau of Belgium at bay, Germany threatening with a bayonet.

M.C. Gallant little Belgium.

*During the last chorus of the song there is a mime of recruiting.
The men hand in their pierrot huts und kiss the girls goodbye,
marching off behind the screen.*
*They re-emerge wearing uniform caps and marching off
saluting.*

NEWSPANEL. COURAGE WILL BRING US VICTORY.

BAND.   CAVALRY CHARGE MUSIC

*Six men, wearing the capes and caps of the French cavalry
enter upstage, riding imaginary horses.*

STANDARD-BEARER. Bonjour, mes amis.
FRENCH SOLDIER. Bonjour, mon capitaine.
STANDARD-BEARER. Il fait beau pour la chasse . . . Vive la
République!
FRENCH OFFICER. En avant!

*They gallop downstage. There is a sound of gunfire: an ambush.
They retreat.*

STANDARD-BEARER. Maintenant, mes amis!
FRENCH OFFICER. Ah oui.
STANDARD-BEARER. Pour la gloire.
FRENCH OFFICER. Charge!

BAND.   PART OF THE MARSEILLAISE

*The cavalry charge. There is a sound of machine-gun fire and
whinnying horses. The men are killed and collapse.*
*They hold their poses, standing, sitting or lying while a girl
singer enters.*

NEWSPANEL. GERMANS HELD AT LIÈGE . . . LONDON
WILD WITH JOY.

SONG.   BELGIUM PUT THE KIBOSH ON THE KAISER

A silly German sausage
Dreamt Napoleon he'd be,
Then he went and broke his promise,
It was made in Germany.
He shook hands with Britannia
And eternal peace he swore,
Naughty boy, he talked of peace
While he prepared for war.
He stirred up little Serbia
To serve his dirty tricks
But naughty nights at Liège
Quite upset this Dirty Dick.
His luggage labelled 'England'
And his programme nicely set,
He shouted 'First stop Paris',
But he hasn't got there yet.

For Belgium put the kibosh on the Kaiser;
Europe took a stick and made him sore;
On his throne it hurts to sit,
And when John Bull starts to hit,
He will never sit upon it any more.

His warships sailed upon the sea,
They looked a pretty sight
But when they heard the bulldog bark
They disappeared from sight.
The Kaiser said 'Be careful,
If by Jellicoe they're seen,
Then every man-of-war I've got
Will be a submarine'.
We chased his ships to Turkey,
And the Kaiser startled stood,
Scratch'd his head and said 'Don't hurt,
You see I'm touching wood';

Then Turkey brought her warships
Just to aid the German plot,
Be careful, Mr Turkey,
Or you'll do the Turkey Trot.

Belgium put the kibosh on the Kaiser;
Europe took a stick and made him sore;
And if Turkey makes a stand
She'll get ghurka'd and japanned,
And it won't be Hoch the Kaiser any more.

He'll have to go to school again
And learn his geography,
He quite forgot Britannia
And the hands across the sea,
Australia and Canada,
The Russian and the Jap,
And England looked so small
He couldn't see her on the map.
Whilst Ireland seemed unsettled,
'Ah' said he 'I'll settle John',
But he didn't know the Irish
Like he knew them later on.
Though the Kaiser stirred the lion,
Please excuse him from the crime,
His lunatic attendant
Wasn't with him at the time.

The cavalry rise and join in. All sing:

Belgium put the kibosh on the Kaiser;
Europe took a stick and made him sore;
We shall shout with victory's joy,
Hold your hand out, naughty boy,
You must never play at soldiers any more.

> For Belgium put the kibosh on the Kaiser;
> Europe took a stick and made him sore;
> On his throne it hurts to sit,
> And when John Bull starts to hit,
> He will never sit upon it any more.

All go off, except for one French officer who sits on stage writing a letter.

NEWSPANEL. BRUSSELS FALLS.

FRENCH OFFICER. The battlefield is unbelievable; heaps of corpses, French and German, lying everywhere, rifles in hand. Thousands of dead lying in rows on top of each other in an ascending arc from the horizontal to an angle of sixty degrees. The guns recoil at each shot; night is falling and they look like old men sticking out their tongues and spitting fire. The rain has started, shells are bursting and screaming; artillery fire is the worst. I lay all night listening to the wounded groaning. The cannonading goes on; whenever it stops we hear the wounded crying from all over the woods. Two or three men go mad every day.

The French officer goes off. A German officer is discovered on the opposite side of the stage, reading a letter.

GERMAN OFFICER. Nothing more terrible could be imagined; we advanced much too fast. The men are desperately tired. I feel great pity for many of the civilian population, who have lost everything, but they hate us. One of them fired at us; he was immediately taken out and shot. Yesterday we were ordered to attack the enemy flank in a forest of beeches, but the enemy gunners saw us and opened fire; the men were done for, the shells fell like hail.

He goes off. Three men dressed as Tommies in full kit enter and march diagonally across the stage. They are followed by four pierrots wearing straw boaters, and shouldering walking-sticks instead of rifles. The three soldiers sing. As they sing, the pierrots go haltingly through the motions of arms drill with their sticks.

SONG.   ARE WE DOWNHEARTED ?

> Are we downhearted ? No.
> Then let your voices ring and all together sing,
> Are we downhearted ? No.
> Not while Britannia rules the waves, not likely;
> While we have Jack upon the sea, and Tommy on the land
> we needn't fret.
> It's a long, long way to Tipperary, but we're not down-
> hearted yet.

SONG.   HOLD YOUR HAND OUT, NAUGHTY BOY

> Hold your hand out, naughty boy.
> Hold your hand out, naughty boy.
> Last night, in the pale moonlight,
> I saw you, I saw you;
> With a nice girl in the park,
> You were strolling full of joy,
> And you told her you'd never kissed a girl before:
> Hold your hand out, naughty boy.

BAND.   FEW BARS OF SMASH-UP RAG

Bayonet Drill Sequence: The soldiers go off, leaving the recruits. A sergeant-major enters and instructs them in bayonet drill. He speaks in an incomprehensible garbled language. What he says is roughly as follows. Occasional words can be made out and these are printed in italics:

Now, you lousy lot, we're going to learn rifle drill and bayonet practice. I'm going to teach you how to handle a rifle and fix bayonets. – Your rifle is your best friend and I'm going to be your worst bloody enemy. First thing, get your rifle on your left shoulder, left hand parallel to the ground, right hand down the seam of your trousers. First

Ruin his chances!

move your right hand smartly across your body, grabbing
the rifle at the point of balance, and bring your rifle down
between your knees. You at the end there I'll have your
bloody *guts* for *garters* in a minute. Now then, with the rifle
in that position you come to the bayonet fix. BAYONET!!
FIX!! With right hand hold rifle six inches from the top,
the first six inches don't count. Right – BAYONET –
ONE! TWO – bring bayonet down at angle of ninety degrees over the rifle and THREE bring the bayonet down
over the bayonet catch. BAYONET . . . Wait for it . . .
Bayonet, by numbers, one – two – three –Fix.

*One recruit cannot find his bayonet – the Sergeant-Major
approaches him.*

Hello, hello, hello, hello. Where's your bayonet ?

*He swears in the recruit's ear. During this, the recruit's rifle has
slipped between his knees.*

Where's your bloody rifle – gone now ? Standing on parade like
some fancy *fairy !*

*He pulls the rifle out from between the recruit's legs and the
recruit places the bayonet quickly on his rifle.*

Now then, next position is the lunge. Bring the rifle up
smartly. Right hand on the neck of the butt, left hand at the
point of balance, left foot forward. Right hand behind butt of
rifle to give it a thrust. In – out – on guard! and don't poke
about there like you're poking a bleeding fire either. Now
get your right foot firmly balanced or you'll fall flat on your
arse. Now when he's coming at you with a lunge – 'cos he's
also joined the bleedin' army – you can do what we call the
left parry. Which is – get the rifle under the swivel butt with
the left hand, and don't bloody ask me what the swivel butt is
here for. Get the right hand under butt of rifle, and swing

over to the left and bash his head in and if that doesn't work, swing into the right parry. Now the right parry is getting the rifle at the point of balance in the left hand – get the right hand on the butt of the rifle and swing into his balls. *Ruin his chances,* and then on, 'cos there's plenty more where he just came from. Now let's start with the right parry. Right parry, by numbers, by the count of three – one – two – three! Come on, get that butt in there. Right, you dress back, you dress back, you dress back . . . You again.

The recruit on the end does it appallingly. The Sergeant-Major beckons the recruit over to him, and starts a tirade.

You're *bloody clever,* you're *bloody smart* you are. I've been in the *Army twenty-five bloody years,* and got *three bloody stripes* to prove it. I suppose you've been to *public school.* And you don't go forward with all those *bloody lah-de-dah and tally-ho's.* You go like this.

The Sergeant does right parry, accompanied by a frightening blood-curdling scream. He orders the recruit to do the same, three times in succession, the recruit screaming and getting very excited.

That's better. Fall in, all of you. I've got eyes in the back of my bloody head. I'm keeping a fatherly eye on you. Right then – get to your positions for bayonet charge, and get that look on your face. You just think of *those bastards out there. Oh my God, look at that !*

Drawing attention to the recruits' insipid faces.

Think of those bastards out there. Up your *mother,* up your *sister,* up your *brother,* too, by the look of some of you. Platoon by numbers – bayonet ! –

Notices recruit's position.

What you got, a bleeding *bow and arrow* there ? CHARGE !

The recruit on the end breaks loose and jumps into the audience, and chases a girl, who screams. The Sergeant calls him back shouting:

Get back here you bloody little *filthy sex maniac.* Your
bloody number's up, mate. Your life won't be worth living
and I don't think you're going to bloody die laughing either.
*Right O, line up, left turn, quick march – left-right-left-right-
left-right.*

Recruits quickly double march off.

I'm very sorry, madam, we were only doing bayonet drill.

*He salutes the woman who screamed, as he goes off. As they
march off a girl singer enters.*
*During the song the following slides are projected, at the points
indicated by numbers in the text:*

Slide 13: 1914 poster – 'Women of Britain say – "GO" '.
*Slide 14: 1914 poster – 'Everyone should do his bit – Enlist now'
depicting a Boy Scout in uniform.*
*Slide 15: 1914 poster – 'Which? Have you a REASON –
or only an EXCUSE – for not enlisting NOW?'*
*Slide 16: 1914 poster – ' "Stand not upon the order of your going
but go at once" – Shakespeare – Macbèth 3.4. Enlist now.'*
*Slide 17: Poster – 'Who's absent? Is it YOU?' – depicting a line
of soldiers with John Bull in the foreground pointing accusingly
à là Kitchener.*

SONG.   I'LL MAKE A MAN OF YOU

> The Army and the Navy need attention, [13]
> The outlook isn't healthy you'll admit,
> But I've got a perfect dream of a new recruiting scheme,
> Which I think is absolutely it.
> If only other girls would do as I do
> I believe that we could manage it alone,
> For I turn all suitors from me but the sailor and the
>   Tommy,
> I've an army and a navy of my own.

On Sunday I walk out with a Soldier,
On Monday I'm taken by a Tar,
On Tuesday I'm out with a baby Boy Scout, [14]
On Wednesday a Hussar;
On Thursday I gang oot wi' a Scottie,
On Friday, the Captain of the crew;
But on Saturday I'm willing, if you'll only take the shilling,
To make a man of any one of you. [15]

I teach the tenderfoot to face the powder,
That gives an added lustre to my skin,
And I show the raw recruit how to give a chaste salute,
So when I'm presenting arms he's falling in.
It makes you almost proud to be a woman.
When you make a strapping soldier of a kid.
And he says 'You put me through it and I didn't want to
   do it
But you went and made me love you so I did.' [16]

Three girls enter in revealing 'military' costumes and join in.

On Sunday I walk out with a Bo'sun.
On Monday a Rifleman in green,
On Tuesday I choose a 'sub' in the 'Blues',
On Wednesday a Marine;
On Thursday a Terrier from Tooting,
On Friday a Midshipman or two,
But on Saturday I'm willing, if you'll only take the shilling,
To make a man of any one of you.

The band repeat the chorus.

SINGER. Come on, boys; we need a million.
FIRST GIRL. A million.
SINGER. Be a man; enlist today.
SECOND GIRL. Enlist today.
SINGER. Have you a man digging your garden, when he should
   be digging trenches?

But on Saturday I'm willing, if you'll only take the shilling,
To make a man of any one of you!

THIRD GIRL. He should be digging trenches.

SINGER. Have we any able-bodied men in the house? (*Then picking up the last lines of the chorus:*)

> . . . But on Saturday I'm willing, if you'll only take the shilling,
> To make a man of any one of you. [17]

All go off.
An army driver comes on and sets stools, etc., for car seats. Field-Marshal Sir John French and his aide-de-camp and Field-Marshal Sir Henry Wilson enter. They take their places in the 'car'.

NEWSPANEL. THE ALLIES CONFER.

FRENCH. Right driver . . . steady on there! One must always remember the class of people these French generals come from.

AIDE. Yes, sir.

FRENCH. Mostly tradesmen. Shan't understand a damn word they say, anyway.

WILSON. With regard to that, sir, do you think I ought to organize an interpreter.

FRENCH. Don't be ridiculous, Wilson; the essential problem at the moment is we must have the utmost secrecy.

General Lanrezac, his aide and General de Moranneville enter.

LANREZAC. Où sont les Anglais?

MORANNEVILLE. Yes, mon Général, it is your turn to wait now.

LANREZAC. Qu'est-ce qu'il dit le Belge?

FRENCH AIDE. Les Anglais, nous les avons attendu longtemps.

MORANNEVILLE. Decisive action by Britain and France while my troops were holding the Germans at Liège, and the war would have been over by now.

LANREZAC. En français Belgique.

WILSON. I've actually worked out the number of carriages

we'll need for the first stage, sir, and even the amount of forage for the horses; wouldn't care to see the figures, would you?

FRENCH. No. Not just now, thank you.

WILSON. I thought that considering the terrain . . .

FRENCH. Yes, we know all about your bicycle trips round France, Wilson.

They arrive and disembark.

WILSON. My dear Lanrezac, how simply splendid to see you again.

LANREZAC. (*French gibberish.*)

WILSON. May I present to you Field-Marshal, Sir John French, Commander-in-Chief of the British Expeditionary Force.

LANREZAC. (*French gibberish.*)

FRENCH. How do you do, sir?

LANREZAC. (*French gibberish.*)

FRENCH AIDE. May I present General de Moranneville, Commander-in-Chief of the Belgian Forces.

FRENCH. Ah yes; splendid, gallant little Belgium, what?

LANREZAC. (*French gibberish.*)

FRENCH. What?

FRENCH AIDE (*translating*). You are here, my General, and not a moment too soon.

FRENCH. Damn it all, we came here as quickly as we could; you have damn bad roads in France.

LANREZAC. (*French gibberish.*)

FRENCH AIDE (*translating*). If we are beaten, we owe it to you. God knows where you have been.

FRENCH. Well, damn it, we're under no obligation, are we?

Lanrezac and his aide talk together in French.

WILSON. I say, sir, do you think we ought to have an interpreter?

FRENCH. Certainly not, Wilson. I can handle this perfectly well on my own, thank you. (*To Lanrezac.*) Mon Général, promenade s'il vous plaît ?

LANREZAC. (*French gibberish.*)

French signals to his aide for a map. The aide brings it.

FRENCH. What ? – Yes. Excusez-moi, s'il vous plaît. Merci – thank you. (*To Lanrezac.*) Mon Général, Les Allemands . . .

LANREZAC. On écoute, les allemands, mon Général.

FRENCH. Yes, of course; Les allemands traverser . . . (*To aide.*) What's 'cross the river' ?

WILSON. Traverser le fleuve.

FRENCH. Yes, yes, of course. (*To Lanrezac.*) Traverser le fleuve . . . ici . . . ahoy, à Hoy.

LANREZAC. Ah oui, ah oui.

FRENCH. Yes, yes . . . Ahoy.

LANREZAC. Non, à Huy, à Huy.

FRENCH. Yes, Ahoy.

LANREZAC. Huy.

FRENCH. What ?

WILSON. No, no, no; pardonnez-moi. Les allemands traverser le fleuve à Huy, n'est-ce pas ?

LANREZAC. (*French gibberish.*)

FRENCH AIDE. My General thinks, monsieur, that the Germans have come to the river to fish.

FRENCH. To fish ?

AIDE. They've come to the river to fish, sir.

WILSON. I think he means, sir, that the Germans will, in fact, cross the river at the bridge.

FRENCH. Oh, yes, of course. Très bon, très bon. In that case gentlemen, we will hold one division, un division, guarding the bridge – les ponts, là, and another division will be held in reserve by the clump of trees, le clump of trees, là, and the French Cavalry will govern the sector from there to there. Là, là!!

LANREZAC. Là et là!!! La cavalerie française, elle est là?
(*French gibberish.*)

FRENCH. Yes, but damn it, we only have four divisions instead
of six promised by Kitchener. The English Cavalry must be
held in reserve.

FRENCH AIDE. When may we expect the forces of the B.E.F.
to come into action?

LANREZAC. Le B.E.F., mon Général.

FRENCH. All in good time, as soon as possible . . . the 24th.

LANREZAC. Vingt-quatre, oui . . . (*French gibberish.*)

FRENCH AIDE. Does the general think the Germans will wait
until we sew on the last button?

LANREZAC. (*French gibberish.*)

FRENCH. Damn it all, Wilson, this is no way to conduct a conference!

WILSON. What?

FRENCH. We're not here under any obligation.

MORANNEVILLE. May I remind both gentlemen that my
country has already fallen. So far, to help us, we have re-
ceived the visit of one staff officer, to observe. Decisive
action by Britain and France, while my troops were holding
Liège and the war would have been over by now. Adieu,
gentlemen. (*He goes off.*)

FRENCH. Whatever our chaps can do, they'll do . . .

Aide gives a medal to French.

Mon Général, I have been entrusted by His Majesty, the
King, to help you in your hour of need.

He presents the medal to Lanrezac.

LANREZAC. (*French gibberish.*)

Lanrezac presents a medal to French.

Pour le Belge.

He gives a medal to his aide.

Mon Général . . .

The French group go off. Four French girls enter with wine and flowers which they present to the British officers.

GIRLS. Les anglais!! Bienvenu, monsieur!

BAND.   MADEMOISELLE FROM ARMENTIÈRES

As the officers go, British privates come on and dance off with the girls.

NEWSPANEL. AUG 25 RETREAT FROM MONS. AUG 30 FIRST BRITISH WOUNDED ARRIVE AT WATERLOO.

FIRST WOMAN (*an off-stage voice*). Lovely violets . . .

SECOND WOMAN. Star, News, Standard . . . First wounded arrive at Waterloo . . . Read all about it.

FIRST WOMAN. Lovely violets . . .

SECOND WOMAN. Star, News, Standard . . . First wounded arrive from France.

A Sergeant and wounded soldiers come on.

SERGEANT. Come on then, let's have you. Get yourselves fell in. Mind your crutch . . . get moving.

FIRST SOLDIER. No flags, sarg?

SERGEANT. No.

FIRST SOLDIER. Waterloo, boys, can you smell it?

SERGEANT. Get yourselves in a straight line. (*Officers and nurse enter.*) Eyes front.

FIRST SOLDIER. They can't do that, can they, sarg? They haven't got any.

FIRST OFFICER. Thank you, sergeant, carry on.

A corporal enters.

SERGEANT. Yes, corporal?

CORPORAL. Ambulances are ready, sarg. Officers only.

SERGEANT. What about the other ranks?

CORPORAL. No arrangements made for them at the moment.

SERGEANT. All right, carry on, corporal. (*Exit Corporal. To officers*.) Excuse me, sir, if you care to step this way we have transport laid on for you.

FIRST OFFICER. Nearly home, George. Thank you, sergeant.

SECOND SOLDIER. Sir, sir, Higgins, sir, B Company.

FIRST OFFICER. Hallo, Higgins.

SECOND SOLDIER. Better than up the old Salient, eh, sir ?

FIRST OFFICER. Indeed yes, good journey home ?

SECOND SOLDIER. Yes, thank you, sir.

FIRST OFFICER. Chin up then. See you back at the front.

(*Exit.*)

SECOND SOLDIER. Yes, sir.

FIRST SOLDIER (*to the nurse, who has been talking to the second officer and is helping him off*.) You're wasting your time with him, darling, it's in splints.

SERGEANT. That's enough out of you.

SECOND SOLDIER. What about us then, sarg ?

SERGEANT. I'm waiting further orders.

The soldiers begin softly singing 'WE'RE 'ERE BECAUSE WE'RE 'ERE', *getting louder.*

We're 'ere because we're 'ere, because we're 'ere, because we're 'ere,

We're 'ere because we're 'ere, because we're 'ere, because we're 'ere –

SERGEANT. All right, cut it out.

GEORGE. What about a train back then, sarg ?

SERGEANT. You'll get that soon enough.

Corporal enters.

FIRST SOLDIER. Mafeking's been relieved, sarg.

SERGEANT. All right – corporal.

CORPORAL. All arranged, sarg. Some lorry drivers outside have volunteered to take the men to Millbank Hospital in their dinner hour.

SERGEANT. Thank you, corporal, carry on . . . All right, men,

Pack up your troubles in your old kit bag,
And smile, smile, smile . . .

get yourselves fell in. We've got transport laid on for you. Come on now, pick 'em up, keep smiling, you're out of the war now.

NURSE (*to stretcher case*). Don't worry, we'll have you back in the firing line within a week.

WOUNDED SOLDIERS (*singing as they march off*):

Pack up your troubles in your old kit bag and smile, smile, smile,

While you've a lucifer to light your fag,

Smile boys that's the style. . . .

NEWSPANEL. 300,000 ALLIED CASUALTIES DURING AUGUST.

They go off, leaving the Sergeant and Corporal. A girl singer comes on with tray of bonbons etc. and offers them.

Slide 18 is projected and the following sequence during the song:

Slide 18: Poster – 'Carters's Little Liver Pills – for Active Service. For the Keen Eye of Perfect Health. Biliousness, Torpid Liver and Constipation.' Depicting a recruit stripped to the waist being examined by a Doctor.

Slide 19: Advertisement –'PHOSFERINE The Greatest of All Tonics, Royalty Use Phosferine as a Liver Tonic, Blood Enricher, Nerve Strengthener.'

Slide 20: Advertisement – 'Beware of umbrellas made on German frames. When you Buy an Umbrella Insist on Having a Fox's frame. Entirely British made. Look for these Marks. S. FOX & CO. LIMITED. PARAGON'.

Slide 21: Advertisement – 'IF YOU ARE RUN DOWN, TAKE BEECHAM'S PILLS'. Depicting a cyclist, who has just been run down by another cyclist.

GIRL. Chocolates, vanilla ices, bonbons; next week at this theatre, a special double bill: the great American comedy Teddy Get Your Gun and He Didn't Want to Do It, featuring Whata Funk, the conchie. Chocolates, vanilla ices, bonbons. (*Enter male dancer with sheet music.*) Have you got your copy of Gwendoline Brogden's latest hit – complete with pianoforte and banjo parts included –

SONG.   HITCHY-KOO

> Oh! Every evening hear him sing,
> It's the cutest little thing,
> With the cutest little swing,
> Hitchy-koo, Hitchy-koo. [19]

> Oh, simply meant for Kings and Queens,
> Don't you ask me what it means,
> I just love that Hitchy-koo,
> Hitchy-koo, Hitchy-koo.

> Say he does it just like no-one could,
> When he does it say he does it good,
> Oh, every evening hear him sing
> It's the cutest little thing
> With the cutest little swing,
> Hitchy-koo, Hitchy-koo. [20]

Band verse: Dance routine [21].

> Say he does it just like no-one could
> When he does it say he does it good.
> Oh, every evening hear him sing,
> It's the cutest little thing,
> With the cutest little swing,
> Hitchy-koo, Hitch-koo, Hitchy-koo. . . .

As the singer and partner go off, six British soldiers come on, whistling and humming 'Hitchy-koo'. They set up signs reading 'Piccadilly' (a fingerpost), 'Conducted tours of the German trenches', 'Apply to G.H.Q. 20 miles to the rear'. They settle within the area of the trench marked off by the signs, playing cards, writing, playing a mouth organ, etc.

NEWSPANEL. TRENCH WARFARE BEGINS . . . THE FIRST WINTER.

Hitchy-koo

FIRST SOLDIER. Want a game? Here you are, you're banker.

The soldier with the mouth organ plays 'Clementine'.

SECOND SOLDIER. Yes.

THIRD SOLDIER. Oi!

FOURTH SOLDIER. Sorry, mate.

SECOND SOLDIER. What's he doing?

THIRD SOLDIER. Writing to his lady love.

SECOND SOLDIER. Oh blimey! Not again.

THIRD SOLDIER. Third volume. My dearest, I waited for you for two hours last night at Hellfire Corner, but you didn't turn up. Can it be that you no longer love me? Signed – Harry Hotlips.

SECOND SOLDIER. What's she like?

FOURTH SOLDIER. Lovely.

SECOND SOLDIER: Is she?

THIRD SOLDIER. Bet she's got a nose like a five inch shell.

FOURTH SOLDIER. Shut up, will you? I'm trying to concentrate.

FIFTH SOLDIER. You writing for that paper again?

FOURTH SOLDIER. Yes, they don't seem to realize they're in at the birth of the Wipers Gazette. Here, do you want to hear what I've written?

SECOND SOLDIER. No.

FOURTH SOLDIER (*to fifth*). Do you want to hear it?

FIFTH SOLDIER. Yes, go on.

FOURTH SOLDIER. The Wipers Gazette. Agony Column. Do you believe good news in preference to bad? Do you think the war will be over by spring-time? Have you got faith in our generals? If the answer to any of these questions is yes, then you are suffering from that dread disease, Optimism, and should take seven days' leave immediately.

FIRST SOLDIER. Wish you'd take ten.

FIFTH SOLDIER. Not a bad idea that paper.

SECOND SOLDIER. No, you want to get it framed.

They don't seem to realize they're in at the birth of the
Wipers Gazette

FIFTH SOLDIER. Yea, put one in for me. Now the winter nights are drawing in, wanted, cure for trench feet, corns, gripes . . .

FIRST SOLDIER. Black or white?

FIFTH SOLDIER. . . . chilblains, and how about some letters an' all – put that in.

THIRD SOLDIER. How about some Christmas parcels and all – put that in!

FIRST SOLDIER (*to sixth*). What's up with you, got company?

SIXTH SOLDIER. Yea, last time I went down to that delousing station, they only shoved a hot iron over my trousers, came out with more than I went in with.

Sound of distant bombardment.

FIFTH SOLDIER. Hey listen.

THIRD SOLDIER. Yea. They're copping it down Railway Wood tonight.

SIXTH SOLDIER. No, that's Hill Sixty.

FIFTH SOLDIER. No, not that. Listen.

German soldiers are heard singing in the distance.

SONG.   HEILIGE NACHT

>Stille Nacht, heilige nacht,
>Alles schläft, einsam wacht,
>Nur das traute hochheilige Paar.
>Holder Knabe im lokkigen Haar,
>Schlaf' in himmlischer Ruh!
>Schlaf' in himmlischer Ruh!

SECOND SOLDIER (*as the Germans sing*). What is it?

FIFTH SOLDIER. Singing.

THIRD SOLDIER. It's those Welsh bastards in the next trench.

FIFTH SOLDIER. It's Jerry that is.

FIRST SOLDIER. It's an 'ymn.

SIXTH SOLDIER. No – it's a carol.

SECOND SOLDIER. Wouldn't have thought they had them.

THIRD SOLDIER. It's Jerry all right, it's coming from over there.

FOURTH SOLDIER. Sings well for a bastard, doesn't he?

FIRST SOLDIER. Sing up, Jerry, let's hear you!

FIFTH SOLDIER. Put a sock in it, let's listen.

They listen as 'Heilige Nacht' finishes.

SECOND SOLDIER. Nice, wasn't it? Good on you, mate!

GERMAN SOLDIER. Hallo, Tommy! . . . Hallo, Tommy!

FOURTH SOLDIER. He heard you.

SECOND SOLDIER. Hallo!

GERMAN SOLDIER. Wie gehts?

FIRST SOLDIER. Eh?

GERMAN SOLDIER. How are you, I am very well thank you, good night.

FIRST SOLDIER. That's another day gone!

GERMAN SOLDIER. Hey, Tommy. How is it with you?

ENGLISH SOLDIERS. Lovely! Very good! – etc.

THIRD SOLDIER. Guten singing, Jerry!

SECOND SOLDIER. Got any more?

GERMAN SOLDIER. Fröhliche Weinacht!

ENGLISH SOLDIERS. Eh?

GERMAN SOLDIER. Good . . . Happy Christmas!

SECOND SOLDIER. Happy Christmas!

FIRST SOLDIER. Hey! It's Christmas!

FOURTH SOLDIER. No. Tomorrow.

SECOND SOLDIER (*to first soldier*). What about opening your parcel?

FIRST SOLDIER. I forgot it was Christmas.

GERMAN SOLDIER. Hallo, Tommy!

ENGLISH SOLDIERS. Yea?

GERMAN SOLDIER. It is for you now to sing us a good song for Christmas, ja?

ENGLISH SOLDIERS. Oh, ja!

THIRD SOLDIER. Let's give them one.

SECOND SOLDIER. Go on, then!

THIRD SOLDIER. I can't sing.

FIRST SOLDIER. We know that.

FOURTH SOLDIER. Who's going to sing it, then?

THIRD SOLDIER (*to first*). Give them that one of yours.

FIRST SOLDIER. What – Cookhouse?

ENGLISH SOLDIERS. Yeah!!

FIRST SOLDIER. All right, Jerry, get down in your dugouts – it's coming over!

He sings.

SONG.   CHRISTMAS DAY IN THE COOKHOUSE

It was Christmas day in the cookhouse,
The happiest day of the year,
Men's hearts were full of gladness
And their bellies full of beer,
When up spoke Private Shorthouse,
His face as bold as brass,
Saying, 'We don't want your Christmas pudding
You can stick it up your . . .'

ALL. Tidings of comfort and joy, comfort and joy,
Oh, tidings of comfort and joy!

FIRST SOLDIER. It was Christmas day in the harem,
The eunuchs were standing round,
And hundreds of beautiful women,
Were stretched out on the ground,
When in strode the Bold Bad Sultan,
And gazed on his marble halls,
Saying, 'What do you want for Christmas, boys?'
And the eunuchs answered . . .

ALL. Tidings of comfort and joy, comfort and joy,
Oh, tidings of comfort and joy.

Sound of Germans applauding: 'Bravo, Tommy.'

FOURTH SOLDIER. Hey, listen.

GERMAN SOLDIER. Bravo, Tommy. English carols is very beautiful! Hey, Tommy, present for you, coming over!

ENGLISH SOLDIERS. Watch out! Get down! – etc.

The soldiers dive for cover. A boot is thrown from the darkness upstage and lands in the trench.

THIRD SOLDIER. Quick, put a sandbag on it.

SIXTH SOLDIER. What is it?

FIFTH SOLDIER. It's a boot.

FIRST SOLDIER. Drop it in a bucket of water.

FIFTH SOLDIER. It's a Jerry boot.

THIRD SOLDIER. What's that sticking out of it?

SIXTH SOLDIER. It's a bit of fir tree.

FIRST SOLDIER. A bit of ribbon.

FIFTH SOLDIER. Fags.

FOURTH SOLDIER. What's that?

THIRD SOLDIER. That's chocolate, that is.

SECOND SOLDIER. Is it?

SIXTH SOLDIER. Yeah.

ENGLISH SOLDIERS. Thanks, Jerry – etc.

FIRST SOLDIER. That's German sausage.

SECOND SOLDIER. Is it?

FIRST SOLDIER. Yeah.

SECOND SOLDIER. It's yours.

FIFTH SOLDIER. Eh, we'll have to send them something back, won't we?

SECOND SOLDIER. Here, come on, get your parcel open.

FIRST SOLDIER. Here, what about your one, then?

SECOND SOLDIER. Well, I ain't got one. Here, they can have my Christmas card from Princess Mary . . .

FIRST SOLDIER. Tell you what they can have, the old girl's Christmas pudding. Bet they've never tasted anything like that before.

FIRST SOLDIER. Here you are, I've been saving this. They can have my tin of cocoa – might help them sleep.

FOURTH SOLDIER. Nothing from me.

FIFTH SOLDIER. Right, Jerry, here's your Christmas box.

He throws the boot.

GERMAN SOLDIER. Thanks, Tommy!

Explosion.

FIRST SOLDIER. Blimey! the Christmas pudding wasn't that bad.

GERMAN SOLDIER. Hey, Tommy! Are you still there?

ENGLISH SOLDIERS. Yeah! No thanks to you – etc.

GERMAN SOLDIER. Many greetings to you, for your many presents and kindnesses to us, we thank you.

SECOND SOLDIER. You're very welcome.

FIRST SOLDIER. That's all right.

GERMAN SOLDIER. Hey, you like to drink with us, ja?

ENGLISH SOLDIERS. Ja!

GERMAN SOLDIER. You like some Schnapps – good Deutsche Schnapps?

FOURTH SOLDIER. Ja!! That's whisky!

ENGLISH SOLDIERS. Yes!

FIRST SOLDIER. Sling it over!

GERMAN SOLDIER. We meet you! Meet you in the middle!

FOURTH SOLDIER. Middle of Piccadilly!

FIRST SOLDIER. See you in the penalty area! Good night, Jerry.

SECOND SOLDIER. Happy New Year, mate!

THIRD SOLDIER. They're marvellous linguists, you know.

SECOND SOLDIER. Oh yes, they learn it at school.

FOURTH SOLDIER. I reckon I'll put that in the Gazette.

FIFTH SOLDIER. What?

FOURTH SOLDIER. About Jerry sending us a present.

FIFTH SOLDIER. Eh! Here! They're coming!

The German soldiers appear upstage.

FIRST GERMAN. Hallo, Tommy.

The third and fifth British soldiers go to meet the Germans.

SECOND GERMAN. Alles gut, ja.

He gives a bottle to the third British soldier.

THIRD SOLDIER. Thanks very much.
SECOND GERMAN. Bitte schön.
FIFTH SOLDIER. Hello, how are you?
THIRD SOLDIER. Merry Christmas.

They shake hands, the others follow.

SECOND SOLDIER. Hello, nice to see you – all right, are you?
'Ere, you should have come over before . . . Stone the
crows, it was him saying good night.

They greet each other.

NEWSPANEL. ALL QUIET ON THE WESTERN FRONT . . .
ALLIES LOSE 850,000 MEN IN 1914 . . . HALF BRITISH
EXPEDITIONARY FORCE WIPED OUT.

*During this message the M.C. enters and the soldiers turn to
watch the newspanel in silence. The soldiers pick up their signs
and go off.*
The M.C. sings 'Goodbye-ee.'

SONG.   GOODBYE-EE

Brother Bertie went away
To do his bit the other day
With a smile on his lips and his
Lieutenant's pips upon his shoulder bright and gay.
As the train moved out he said, 'Remember me to all the
    birds.'
And he wagg'd his paw and went away to war
Shouting out these pathetic words:

Goodbye-ee, goodbye-ee,
Wipe the tear, baby dear, from your eye-ee,
Tho' it's hard to part I know, I'll be tickled to death to go.
Don't cry-ee, don't sigh-ee, there's a silver lining in the sky-ee,
Bonsoir, old thing, cheer-i-o, chin, chin,
Nap-poo, toodle-oo, Goodbye-ee.

The girls come on and join in. The last lines grow fainter as they go off.

Goodbye-ee, goodbye-ee,
Wipe the tear, baby dear, from your eye-ee,
Though it's hard to part I know, I'll be tickled to death to go.
Don't cry-ee, don't sigh-ee, there's a silver lining in the sky-ee . . .

NEWSPANEL. WELCOME 1915 . . . HAPPY YEAR THAT WILL BRING VICTORY AND PEACE.

Sound of shell exploding.
The last line of the song is inaudible.

CURTAIN

Act Two

NEWSPANEL. APRIL 22 . . . BATTLE OF YPRES . . . GER-
MANS USE POISON GAS . . . BRITISH LOSS 59,275
MEN . . . MAY 9 . . . AUBERS RIDGE . . . BRIT-
ISH LOSS 11,619 MEN IN 15 HOURS . . . LAST OF
B.E.F. . . . GAIN NIL. SEPT 25 . . . LOOS . . .
BRITISH LOSS 8,236 MEN IN 3 HOURS . . . GERMAN
LOSS NIL.

The company dressed as pierrots enter and sing.

SONG.   OH IT'S A LOVELY WAR

Oh, oh, oh, it's a lovely war,
Who wouldn't be a soldier, eh?
Oh, it's a shame to take the pay;
As soon as reveille is gone,
We feel just as heavy as lead,
But we never get up till the sergeant
Brings our breakfast up to bed.
Oh, oh, oh, it's a lovely war,
What do we want with eggs and ham,
When we've got plum and apple jam?
Form fours, right turn,
How shall we spend the money we earn?
Oh, oh, oh, it's a lovely war.

Up to your waist in water,
Up to your eyes in slush,
Using the kind of language,

That makes the sergeant blush.
Who wouldn't join the army?
That's what we all inquire;
Don't we pity the poor civilian,
Sitting beside the fire.

Oh, oh, oh, it's a lovely war,
Who wouldn't be a soldier, eh?
Oh, it's a shame to take the pay;
As soon as reveille is gone,
We feel just as heavy as lead,
But we never get up till the sergeant
Brings our breakfast up to bed.
Oh, oh, oh, it's a lovely war,
What do we want with eggs and ham,
When we've got plum and apple jam?
Form fours, right turn,
How shall we spend the money we earn?
Oh, oh, oh, it's a lovely war.

M.C. Ladies and gentlemen, when the Conscription Act was passed, 51,000 able-bodied men left home without leaving any forwarding addresses . . .

Men go off quickly.

GIRLS. Shame!

M.C. . . . and that's in West Ham alone.

As each of the girls speaks her line to the audience she throws a white feather.

FIRST GIRL. Women of England, do your duty, send your men to enlist today!

SECOND GIRL. Have you an able-bodied groom, chauffeur or gamekeeper serving you?

THIRD GIRL. If so, shouldn't he be serving his country?

FOURTH GIRL. Is your best boy in khaki? If not shouldn't he be?

FIFTH GIRL. What did you do in the Great War, Daddy?
GIRLS (*sing*). Oh, oh, oh, it's a lovely,
   Oh, oh, oh, it's a lovely,
   Oh, oh, oh, it's a lovely war!

Girls exeunt.

M.C. Sorry we had to interrupt the War Game in the first half,
   but hostilities took us by surprise; now it's business as usual
   – we'll drum up some char and we'll do part two of the War
   Game. What's the date?
VOICE OFF. August the Twelfth.
M.C. August the Twelfth! Here am I talking to you when
   grouse shooting has commenced. (*Putting on a cloth cap.*)
   Whenever there's a crisis, shoot some grouse, that's what I
   always say. Here we are – part two of the War Game, find
   the biggest profiteer.

NEWSPANEL. 21,000 AMERICANS BECAME MILLIONAIRES
   DURING WAR.

A Scottish ghillie enters, singing a Gaelic song.
He is followed by a grouse-shooting party of British, French,
German, and American munitions manufacturers with a Swiss
banker and beaters.

GHILLIE. It's a beautiful day for a shoot, sir.
GERMANY. Sehr schön – sehr schön.
GHILLIE. Shall we drive them into the guns now, your lord-
   ship?
BRITAIN. Do that for me, Ewan.

The ghillie shouts Gaelic names and abuse.

   Chivvy them along now, Ewan.
GHILLIE. Coming over now, sir.

All shoot grouse and cry with delight, counting the birds they
have shot.

FRANCE. A wonderful year, Bertie.

SWITZERLAND. Highly successful.

BRITAIN. Yes, we still manage to fatten 'em up.

FRANCE. What were you saying about nickel, Von Possehl?

GERMANY. That last consignment – we didn't get it.

FRANCE. Well, we sent it.

GERMANY. Yes, well, you sent us some before, but I mean the latest consignment.

FRANCE. We sent it.

AMERICA. By which route?

FRANCE. Through Holland.

BRITAIN. Aah, there's the fly in the ointment – Holland – very unreliable. The Scandinavian countries are much more convenient.

ALL (*to Germany*). Bad luck – etc.

AMERICA. Hazards of war – loss of consignments.

BRITAIN. Mind you, our navy's a bit to blame on that score, trying to set up a blockade of Germany.

AMERICA. You're telling me. We had three ships stopped by the British Navy last month.

BRITAIN. Well, there you are – it's these unrealistic elements at work – they've just taken Jacks & Co. to court for exporting iron ore to Germany. They've got a blacklist, too – and I'm on it.

GERMANY. My Government want to shoot me.

AMERICA. You're on their shortlist!

BRITAIN. Mind you, they'll never publish it – we bought out some of the papers, you know. Can't break up a union like ours in a few minutes.

GERMANY (*shoots*). Another one for me.

BRITAIN. Well, that's a duck, not a grouse.

GERMANY. Well, I shoot anything.

BRITAIN. So I've noticed. We'll export it to you for fat via Denmark.

GERMANY. When are you going to export some shillings for

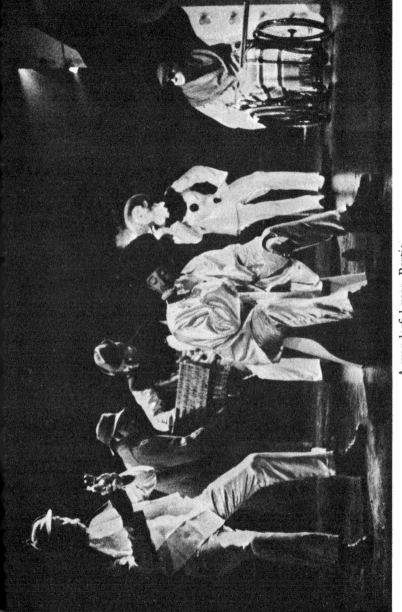

A wonderful year, Bertie

the Krupps fuses you are using in your English grenades?

BRITAIN. All in good time, all in good time . . .

SWITZERLAND. Swiss banks are always open, except in the lunch hour.

AMERICA. Very funny. Look, do you stumblebums realize that there have been two peace scares in the last year? Our shares dropped forty per cent.

FRANCE. What have your exports to Europe in the last three years amounted to? Ten and a half billion dollars.

AMERICA. Yeah, but all we're getting paid in now is your beautifully engraved paper money. That's what we're worried about.

SWITZERLAND. What are you going to do with all that paper money if the Germans win?

BRITAIN. It's no use being the biggest creditor in the world if no one can pay you.

AMERICA. If the U.S. enters the war, that might just finish it.

GERMANY. Now, now, that's very dangerous talk.

BRITAIN. I say, no need to lose your rag.

AMERICA. All right, all right, so long as peace doesn't break out. What about that peace scare in France, Count? Caused a flutter on Wall Street, I can tell you. Have you scotched it?

FRANCE. We flooded our papers with talk of defeatism and shot every pacifist we could find.

AMERICA. Good. I've a cheque for sixty million dollars in my pocket. I want to be able to cash it.

SWITZERLAND. Who is it from?

AMERICA. Russia.

SWITZERLAND. You'll never be able to cash it.

GERMANY. Don't spoil a beautiful day. I have interests in Russia.

GHILLIE. How do you think the war's progressing, sir?

BRITAIN. Oh, not too badly – everything's under control.

GHILLIE. Do you think we'll have peace by Christmas?

AMERICA. Peace?

GERMANY. Peace? Where did he get that story?

FRANCE. War to the finish.

SWITZERLAND. You must understand, my dear fellow, that war is a political and economic necessity.

GHILLIE. Yes, sir, we've six of the family at the front, sir.

BRITAIN. Keeps 'em off the streets.

GHILLIE. That's what my mother says, sir. She's very proud of them, and the allowance helps her and me quite a bit.

AMERICA. Makes men of them.

FRANCE. There will always be a problem of surplus population.

AMERICA. I'm very glad you have due respect for your mother. I'll have you know, keeper, my President is deeply grieved by this war and you can tell your mother this – he regards the whole thing as a tragedy.

BRITAIN. I understand he's a very sick man.

AMERICA. Yes, he's an idealist.

They all drink rapid toasts.

President Wilson!

FRANCE. Président Poincaré!

BRITAIN. The King!

GERMANY. The Kaiser!

AMERICA. He's one of your shareholders, isn't he?

FRANCE. La belle France – our published profit last year was eight million sterling.

They all congratulate him.

BRITAIN. Well done – new springs of wealth arise from war – as the saying goes.

AMERICA. It advances scientific discovery.

FRANCE. War is the life blood of a nation.

GERMANY. Well, I wish you'd tell my Government that; they want to shoot me.

ALL. No, why?

GERMANY. You tell me. My wife, she wore her eyes out, rolling bandages for the boys. I had to buy her spectacles. She never had bad eyes before. Fifty thousand marks I gave to the widows' and orphans' fund.

ALL. What's the trouble, old chap – why do they want to shoot you?

GERMANY. It's my Russian munitions factory.

BRITAIN. Oh yes, how are they doing?

GERMANY. Twenty-four hour shifts. They're turning out bombs and shells all the time.

ALL. Good, well done – etc.

GERMANY. I'm a patriot, but I'm also a businessman; my stock-holders must have dividends. If I didn't make the profits, the Russians would. The people who ought to be shot are those who break international agreements. Germany and France agreed not to bombard the iron-ore works at Briey and Thionville for the duration – and some idiot pilot bombs them. A Frenchman.

AMERICA. What happened to him?

FRANCE. He was court-martialled.

GERMANY. Good.

AMERICA. A hero – eh?

BRITAIN (*finds this very funny*). Rather a shock to be court-martialled, isn't it? Nobody asked questions?

FRANCE. Oh yes – we had delegations, protests – I dealt with them – a hush has fallen. (*All: Bravo!*)

AMERICA. You're smart, Count – you know he got a consignment of barbed wire from Germany through for Verdun only two months before the battle. Isn't that right, Comte?

BRITAIN: You mean the German chappies were caught on their own barbed wire? I say that's a bit near the knuckle, what? Dashed clever, though.

SWITZERLAND. We must take some credit for that.

BRITAIN. Yes, ten per cent, no doubt.

AMERICA. Talking of credit. I promised the guys back home –

and I hope you'll meet them some day – to pass on some of their handouts. (*Hands a card.*) Bethlehem Steel – furnish arms to every quarter of the globe. Cleveland Automatic Machine Company. (*Offers one to Switzerland.*)

SWITZERLAND. Not for me, we're neutral.

AMERICA. It's a recipe for hot chocolate.

(*To Britain*). Hermann Rapide, fires non-stop for fifty hours – we tried to sell these things to the Germans before the war, but they turned us down. Serve 'em right if they lose the war.

GERMANY. Ah, the shrapnel-making machine – you use acids to kill men ?

AMERICA. Four hours it takes, very effective.

GERMANY. You have some pretty good chemists in America, of German extraction, no doubt.

BRITAIN. If it's all the same to you, old boy, we'll stick to the dear old Enfield rifles, cheap and easy to make.

GERMANY (*looking at pamphlet*). No gas ? Ah yes – das grausame stille Tod.

AMERICA. Deadly silent death.

GERMANY. We use phosgene – cylinders 1.4 metres long, highly portable in the trenches – go on a man's back – he can carry a rifle as well.

AMERICA. Look at our arsenal at Edgeworth, Maryland. We've developed sixty-three different poison gases and we've got eight more ready.

BRITAIN. Well, the old chlorine's pretty good. Haig's trying it out this moment at Loos. Mind you, we haven't heard from him. Yet.

All off except the American, who remains in his wheel chair. Voices offstage sing 'Gassed Last Night' as a sequence of slides appear on the screen. The American goes off during the song.

Slide 22: Infantry advancing along the crest of a hill, silhouetted against a large white cloud.

Slide 23: Two German infantrymen running to escape an advancing cloud of poison gas.

Slide 24: A group of 'walking wounded' Tommies, some with bandaged eyes owing to being gassed.

Slide 25: Group of four German soldiers, carrying one of their gassed in a blanket.

Slide 26: Line-up, Indian file, of gassed Tommies, all with bandaged eyes, and one hand on the shoulder of the person immediately in front of them.

Slide 27: Another picture of 'walking wounded': two French Poilus, eyes bandaged, walking hand in hand, escorted by another Frenchman and a Tommy.

Slide 28: Photograph of a German infantryman diving for cover, beside a field gun, as a shell explodes nearby.

Slide 29: Three British infantrymen, full pack, standing in mud and slush, firing over the parapet of a trench.

Slide 30: Three Germans in a dugout, silhouetted against clouds of smoke caused by a plane bombing overhead.

Slide 31: Four Tommies sitting in dugouts, which are merely holes, waist deep in mud.

Slide 32: A dead German soldier, lying in a slit trench.

SONG.   GASSED LAST NIGHT

[22] Gassed last night and gassed the night before, [23]
Going to get gassed tonight if we never get gassed any
    more. [24]
When we're gassed we're sick as we can be,
'Cos phosgene [25] and mustard gas is much too much for
    me.
They're warning [26] us, they're warning us,
One [27] respirator for the four of us.
Thank your lucky stars that three of us can run,
So one of us can use it all alone. [29]

Bombed last night and bombed the night before,
Going to get bombed tonight if we never get bombed any
    more.
When we're bombed we're [29] scared as we can be.
God strafe the bombing planes from High Germany.

They're [30] over us, they're over us,
One shell hole for just the [31] four of us,
Thank your lucky stars there are no more of us,
'Cos [32] one of us could fill it all alone.

A group of five British soldiers enter and build a barricade.

SERGEANT. Get this barricade up, quickly. Keep your heads
down.

LIEUTENANT. Have you got the trench consolidated, sergeant?

SERGEANT. All present and correct, sir.

LIEUTENANT. The C.O. is going to have a word with the men.

SERGEANT. Right, lads – attention!

The Commanding Officer enters.

COMMANDING OFFICER. You can stand the men at ease,
sergeant.

Sound of machine-gun fire. They throw themselves down.

LIEUTENANT. On your feet, lads.

SERGEANT. Come on – jump to it!

COMMANDING OFFICER. You can let them smoke if they want
to.

SERGEANT. The C.O. says you can smoke. But don't let me
catch you.

COMMANDING OFFICER. Now, you men, I've just come from
having a powwow with the colonel; we think you've done
some damn fine work – we congratulate you.

SOLDIERS. Thank you, sir.

COMMANDING OFFICER. I know you've had it pretty hard the
last few days, bombs, shells, and snipers; we haven't escaped

scot-free back at staff either, I can tell you. Anyway, we're all here – well, not all of us, of course; and that gas of ours was pretty nasty – damned wind changing.

LIEUTENANT. Indeed, sir.

COMMANDING OFFICER. But these mishaps do happen in war, and gas can be a war-winning weapon. Anyway, so long as we can all keep smiling; you're white men all. (*To the Lieutenant.*) Sector all tidy now, Lieutenant?

LIEUTENANT. Well, we've buried most of the second Yorks and Lancs, sir; there's a few D.L.I.s and the men from our own company left.

COMMANDING OFFICER. I see. Well, look, let the lads drum up some char. . .

Sound of exploding shell.

LIEUTENANT. Get down, sir.

COMMANDING OFFICER. Good God!

VOICE (*offstage*). Stretcher bearers! . . . Stretcher bearers! . . .

COMMANDING OFFICER. You have no stretcher bearers over there?

LIEUTENANT. No, I'm afraid they went in the last attack, sir. I'm waiting for reliefs from H.Q.

COMMANDING OFFICER. Oh well, they're stout chaps!

Explosion.

COMMANDING OFFICER. Yes, you'd better let the men keep under cover.

LIEUTENANT. Thank you, sir.

COMMANDING OFFICER. Damn place still reeks of decomposing bodies.

LIEUTENANT. I'm afraid it's unavoidable, sir; the trench was mainly full of Jerries.

COMMANDING OFFICER. Yes, of course, you were more or less sharing the same front line for a couple of days, weren't you?

LIEUTENANT. Yes, sir.

COMMANDING OFFICER. Oh well, carry on.

LIEUTENANT. Thank you, sir.

COMMANDING OFFICER. Ye Gods! What's that?

LIEUTENANT. Oh, it's a Jerry, sir.

COMMANDING OFFICER. What?

LIEUTENANT. It's a leg, sir.

COMMANDING OFFICER. Well, get rid of it, man. You can't have an obstruction sticking out of the parapet like that.

He goes off.

LIEUTENANT. Hardcastle. Remove the offending limb.

SERGEANT. Well, we can't do that, sir; it's holding up the parapet. We've just consolidated the position.

LIEUTENANT. Well, get a shovel and hack it off; and then dismiss the men.

He goes off.

SERGEANT. Right, sir. What the bloody hell am I going to hang my equipment on now. All right, lads, get back, get yourselves some char. Heads, trunks, blood all over the place, and all he's worried about is a damned leg.

The soldiers go off.

NEWSPANEL. EASTER 1916 . . . REBELLION IN IRELAND.

The stage is set for an official reception at a 'Palm Court'.

A motionless figure dressed in black, with a jardinière containing pampas-grass on his head, acts both as a piece of furniture and a major-domo.

A lady and a gentleman enter and sing a chorus of the song 'Roses of Picardy'. They form a static tableau, as for a period photograph.

BAND.   WALTZ: LONG, LONG TRAIL

Applause.

The guests enter, dancing. They include Sir John French, Sir Douglas and Lady Haig, Sir William Robertson, Sir Henry Wilson and other army officers with their ladies.

As the guests come downstage in pairs for a series of brief dialogues, their names are announced.

The actresses, with the exception of the actress playing Lady Haig, use their own names, with appropriate titles.

The scene consists of a series of conversation pieces, emerging from and merging back into the general conversation and dancing.

FIRST OFFICER (*the gentleman singer*). Shall we?

MAJOR-DOMO. Sir John French, Commander-in-Chief of His Majesty's Forces. Miss Fanny Carby.

FANNY. Isn't that Sir Douglas Haig – the new man?

FRENCH. Yes. Damned upstart. That other blighter Robertson's here, too.

FANNY. Intrigue upon intrigue.

FRENCH. Hold your tongue, Fanny.

MAJOR-DOMO. Sir William Robertson, The Honorable Barbara Windsor.

BARBARA. I was so thrilled to hear of your new appointment, Willy.

ROBERTSON. One takes these things as they come, you know, Babsy.

BARBARA. Sir Henry Wilson's green with envy.

ROBERTSON. Quite.

BARBARA. He's just behind us, dancing with that frump, Lady Valerie.

MAJOR-DOMO. Sir Henry Wilson, The Lady Valerie Walsh-Jankel.

WILSON. The mess was vastly relieved when they changed their name from Wettin to Windsor.

VALERIE. They're still Germans, Sir Henry.

WILSON. But it's very unpatriotic to say so, Lady Valerie.

Intrigue upon intrigue

MAJOR-DOMO. Sir Douglas and Lady Haig.

HAIG. Canter in the row tomorrow before breakfast, Doris?

LADY HAIG. Don't forget your fitting, Douglas, the new boots.

HAIG. And we're lunching at No. 10 – without French.

LADY HAIG. Congratulations, my dear.

VALERIE. What on earth do they see in him.

WILSON. Shoots pheasant with the Prince of Wales. Lady Doris was one of Queen Alexandra's maids of honour.

VALERIE. Really! What?

WILSON. So now he has the ear of the King, of course.

FANNY. Haig! Sir Douglas Haig! The name rings a bell.

FRENCH. Whisky.

FANNY (*stops in her tracks*). Trade!

FRENCH. 'Fraid so.

The dance ends with a swirl. The men get together in clumps and guffaw over dirty jokes. The women talk in groups.

ROBERTSON. Toby Rawlinson!

RAWLINSON. You have the better of me.

ROBERTSON. Karachi!

RAWLINSON. Polo ponies!

ROBERTSON. Do excuse me.

RAWLINSON. Certainly.

BARBARA. Well, I've volunteered for the V.A.D.

VALERIE. Really? What?

BARBARA. The uniform is so becoming.

Sir John French turns towards Robertson, who arrives back with a drink.

ROBERTSON. Haven't had an opportunity to talk, sir, since my appointment was announced, but I'd like to say how proud I am to serve under you . . .

French turns his back on him. Hushed reaction.

FRENCH (*mutters*). Like to talk to my officers without interruption sometimes.

RAWLINSON. Rather, what!

ROBERTSON. May I take you home, Babsy?

Barbara cries.

RAWLINSON. Good night, Sir John. Ball's in your court, Wilson.

FIRST LADY (*the singer*). What was all that about?

FANNY. Sir John thinks Sir Henry is the perfect man for the job.

FIRST LADY. Sir Henry Wilson?

VALERIE (*aside to Lady Haig*). Keeps him waiting like a lackey.

FRENCH. A word in your private ear, Wilson.

WILSON. Yes, sir.

FRENCH. Now do take that sour expression off your face.

WILSON. I've always understood from you, sir, that the job was mine.

FRENCH. Well, it's your own fault. You're such a brute. You'll never be nice to people you don't like. Anyhow, the day's by no means lost. You'll have to make love to Asquith when you meet him.

WILSON. I'm too suspicious of Kitchener and Churchill to make love to anyone – anyway Asquith hates me – none of them are friends of yours either; you know that, of course.

FRENCH. Oh yes, quite. Anyway, I'm showing them the sort of man I am. Giving Robertson the position I marked down for you. I've refused to mess with him – pretty good, what? Snubbing him just now in the middle of the room.

WILSON. You made your attitude pretty clear, sir.

FRENCH. Well, there you are then. You depend on me. I'm very fond of you, Henry.

WILSON. Thank you, sir.

FRENCH. So keep your pecker up and don't be so gloomy.

VALERIE (*to Wilson*). I wouldn't trust him an inch.

WILSON. I don't.

LADY HAIG (*to the First Officer, the singer*). I will tell you in confidence, my dear, His Majesty very much hopes that my husband will succeed French.

FIRST OFFICER. My God!

LADY HAIG. Yes, oh yes, Douglas thinks French is quite unfitted for the high position he's been called to.

SECOND OFFICER. Who was Sir John's little . . . lady friend?

HAIG. Rank outsider.

SECOND OFFICER. I quite believe it.

HAIG. It's a flaw in his character, you know, his weakness for the fair sex. Loses all sense of decency.

SECOND OFFICER. Really, sir!

HAIG. Yes, well, he had to borrow two thousand pounds from me at Aldershot over a woman.

SECOND OFFICER. Good God, sir!

HAIG. And he was Commander of my Cavalry brigade at the time.

SECOND OFFICER. Damn bad show, sir, borrowing from a subordinate.

HAIG. Appalling!

BAND.   COMRADES

FRENCH. Haig!

HAIG. Sir John!

They advance and shake hands. Applause.

FRENCH. You saw me snub Robertson just now?

HAIG. I did, Sir John.

FRENCH. That's the way to treat 'em.

A photographer comes in and takes a picture.

'Friends in sunshine and shadow' – put that in your photogravure, boy.

PHOTOGRAPHER. The right man in the right job, if I may say so, sir.

FRENCH. You may, you may. Thank you, my man. Well, how did you leave the men at the front, Douglas?

HAIG. Oh, in fine heart, sir, just spoiling for a fight.

FRENCH. Makes one feel very proud. A word in your private ear, Douglas. What do you think of that man Kitchener?

HAIG. Well, sir –

FRENCH. The man's intolerable. He's behaving like a General-issimo now – he's only a damned politician.

HAIG. With regard to that, sir. You know he turned up in Paris in his uniform again.

FRENCH. My God, no! He's no damned right to a uniform at all – I mean Secretary of State for War – what happened?

HAIG. Well, it raised some pretty tricky points of protocol.

FRENCH. Yes, well – what are we going to do about it?

BAND.   WALTZ: APRES LA GUERRE

FANNY. Johnnie.

FRENCH. Excuse me. They're playing my tune. That man Kitchener is more of an enemy to the B.E.F. than Moltke or Ludendorff.

The couples begin waltzing again and gradually go off until only Haig and Lady Haig are left.

VALERIE. How did that man Haig get his pips, if you tell me he failed all his staff college entrance examinations?

WILSON. Duke of Cambridge.

VALERIE. What?

WILSON. Friend of the family.

VALERIE. Oh! yes, on her side.

WILSON. Waived the formalities and let him in.

FRENCH. Yes, well, he may have lent me £2,000, but he made a terrible mess of his field exercises.

SECOND OFFICER (*to Haig*). Good night, sir.

FIRST OFFICER AND LADY (*to Haig*). Good night.

HAIG (*doesn't answer*). That man is a terrible intriguer.

LADY HAIG. Yes, I can tell by his deceitful face.

HAIG. And he's flabby!

LADY HAIG. You've been loyal long enough, my dear.

HAIG. Well, No. 10 tomorrow, Doris.

LADY HAIG. And a field-marshal's job for you.

VOICES OFFSTAGE. My carriage!

Carriages!

Good night!

*Men's voices offstage sing 'Hush, here comes a Whizzbang':
a sequence of slides is projected as follows:*

Slide 33: Night photographs of flares, and various Very lights.

Slide 34: Photograph of a cloud formation.

*Slide 35: Three Tommies walking across duckboards in a muddy
field.*

*Slide 36: Dead Germans lying in a shallow trench in a peaceful-
looking country field.*

*Slide 37: A young French soldier, obviously on burial duty, laden
with wooden crosses.*

Slide 38: Dead French Poilus; one of them has a smile on his face.

*Slide 39: A field with nothing but white wooden crosses as far as
one can see.*

SONG.   HUSH, HERE COMES A WHIZZBANG

(*Tune: 'Hush, here comes the Dream Man'*)

[33] Hush, here comes a whizzbang, [34]
Hush, here comes a whizzbang, [35]
Now, you soldier men, get down those stairs, [36]
Down in your dugouts and say your prayers. [37]
Hush, here comes a whizzbang,
And it's making [38] straight for you,
And you'll see all the wonders [39] of no-man's-land,
If a whizzbang hits you.

HAIG (*entering*). Germany has shot her bolt. The prospects for 1916 are excellent.

BRITISH GENERAL (*entering*). Permission to speak, sir.

HAIG. Of course.

Slide 40: A map of Ypres and the surrounding district, showing Kitchener's Wood, Hill 60, Passchendaele, etc.

BRITISH GENERAL. If we continue in this way, the line of trenches will stretch from Switzerland to the sea. Neither we nor the Germans will be able to break through. The war will end in complete stalemate.

HAIG. Nonsense. We need only one more big offensive to break through and win. My troops are of fine quality, and specially trained for this type of war.

BRITISH GENERAL. This is not war, sir, it is slaughter.

HAIG. God is with us. It is for King and Empire.

BRITISH GENERAL. We are sacrificing lives at the rate of five to sometimes fifty thousand a day.

HAIG. One battle, our superior morale, bombardment.

JUNIOR OFFICER (*entering*). Sir, tell us what to do and we'll do it.

HAIG. We're going to walk through the enemy lines.

British General and Junior Officer go off.

Slide 40 fades into Slide 41: Tommies advancing across no-man's-land, in full battle pack, silhouetted against clouds.
A man's voice, offstage, sings slowly as Haig speaks.

SONG.   THERE'S A LONG, LONG TRAIL

There's a long, long trail a-winding
Into the land of my dreams,
Where the nightingale is singing
And the white moon beams . . .

He carries on humming the tune, ending:

There's a long, long trail a-winding
Into the land of my dreams . . .

. . . till the day when I'll be going down that long, long trail with you.

HAIG (*during the song*). Complete victory . . . the destruction of German militarism . . . victory march on Berlin . . . slow deliberate fire is being maintained on the enemy positions . . . at this moment my men are advancing across no-man's-land in full pack, dressing from left to right; the men are forbidden under pain of court-martial to take cover in any shell hole or dugout . . . their magnificent morale will cause the enemy to flee in confusion . . . the attack will be driven home with the bayonet . . . I feel that every step I take is guided by the divine will.

Sounds of heavy bombardment.

NEWSPANEL. FEBRUARY . . . VERDUN . . . TOTAL LOSS ONE AND A HALF MILLION MEN.

HAIG (*looking through field-glasses*). This is most unsatisfactory. Where are the Sherwood Foresters? Where are the East Lancs on the right?

BRITISH GENERAL (*who has entered during above speech*). Out in No Man's Land.

HAIG. They are sluggish from too much sitting in the trenches.

BRITISH GENERAL. Most of them, sir, will never rise again.

HAIG. We must break through.

BRITISH GENERAL. Regardless of loss, sir?

HAIG. The loss of, say, another 300,000 men may lead to really great results.

BRITISH GENERAL. Yes, sir.

HAIG. And will not impede our ability to continue the offensive. In any case, we have to calculate on another great offensive next year.

BRITISH GENERAL. If the slackers on the Home Front see it our way, sir.

HAIG. Quite.

BRITISH GENERAL. We are rather short of men, sir.

HAIG. What's left?

BRITISH GENERAL. The new chappies from Ireland have just arrived.

HAIG. Rather wild untrained lot! Still, they'll be rearing to have a crack at the Bosche, and what they lack in training, they'll make up for in gallantry.

BRITISH GENERAL. They've just got off the train. Most of them haven't eaten for forty-eight hours—

HAIG. They are moving against a weakened and demoralized enemy. Capture the German line, without further delay.

Six Irish soldiers, wearing green kilts and carrying rifles, enter and stand upstage of Haig and the British General. One soldier is carrying a Union Jack on a pole.

SERGEANT. Right boys, up and at 'em!

ALL. Up the Irish!

Band. Irish Washerwoman.
They dance an attack under bombardment as an Irish jig. They reach their objective and fling themselves down. Birdsong.

SERGEANT. We made it.

FIRST SOLDIER. Where are we, Serg?

SERGEANT. I reckon we've broken into a lull!

SECOND SOLDIER. It's nice, ain't it?

THIRD SOLDIER. Peaceful!

FIRST SOLDIER. Ah, lovely! Look at that.

FOURTH SOLDIER. Aye, Serg, look at that dirty great black mound of earth.

SERGEANT. That's nothing . . . it's an earthwork. We're too near for guns the size o' that to get us. (*Sniper's bullet.*)

THIRD SOLDIER. What was that?

SERGEANT. That must have been a stray one. I should keep under cover if I was you. Trouble is we've been fighting too well. We've arrived ahead of ourselves.

Right boys, up and at 'em!

SECOND SOLDIER. Serg, how many trenches did we capture?

SERGEANT. I reckon about nine.

FIRST SOLDIER. No, ten.

SERGEANT. Make it a round dozen – we'll all be mentioned in despatches for this, you know.

SECOND SOLDIER. Will we be heroes, Serg?

FOURTH SOLDIER. Ah sure, it'll be a great victory for the boys.

Birdsong still continuing.

FIRST SOLDIER. What's that, Serg?

SERGEANT. What's what?

FIRST SOLDIER. Sounds like someone talking over there.

THIRD SOLDIER. Look. It's some Limey wounded in that shell 'ole over there.

SERGEANT. Where?

THIRD SOLDIER. Look! Under that ridge.

SERGEANT. You can't tell the quick from the dead, can you!

FOURTH SOLDIER. They must have fallen in the last attack.

SECOND SOLDIER. What are they blabbering about?

SERGEANT. 'Go back.' 'Go back – you bloody fools'. He's telling us to go back. Thanks, mush.

FIRST SOLDIER. Jesus! That's easier said than done. Eh? You what? He says we're drawing their fire, and to get the flag down. (*Bullet shot.*)

SERGEANT. Seamus, get that flag down.

SECOND SOLDIER. Hey Serg – where did that last one come from?

SERGEANT. I think it must have been our boys!

All but the Sergeant get up and shout upstage.

ALL. Hey, don't shoot. It's us.

SECOND SOLDIER. There's human beings over here.

Heavy gun shell. They all flatten on the ground.

SERGEANT. Now you see what you've done. You bloody idiots. Seamus!

FIFTH SOLDIER. Serg?

SERGEANT. You're the quickest on your pins. Report back to
    H.Q. pronto. Tell the artillery not to waste their shells on
    us, but to save them for Jerry. Tell them to raise their
    bloody sights a bit.

FIFTH SOLDIER. Back through all that?

SERGEANT. Yeah.

FIFTH SOLDIER. On me own?

SERGEANT. Now is it for us to all give ground when we've
    come so near the prize?

FIFTH SOLDIER. No, I see that. I'll tell 'em the battle's been
    won.

SERGEANT. Do that.

Fifth Soldier walks upstage.

FIFTH SOLDIER. Hey Serg, that last one got the bridge.

SECOND SOLDIER. Does that mean we're cut off then?

FIFTH SOLDIER. No, I'll swim for it.

SERGEANT. Give yourself a treat. That'll be the first wash he's
    had this year. Hey, Seamus, bring us back a bottle of
    whisky – Irish! (*Bullet shot.*)

SECOND SOLDIER. He's gone under, Serg.

SERGEANT. What do you mean?

SECOND SOLDIER. They got him.

SERGEANT. Well, who's next? Come on, someone's got to go.

FOURTH SOLDIER. I wouldn't mind a swim, Serg.

SERGEANT. Right then, off you go. Tell them there's hundreds
    stranded on this ridge. . . .

ALL. Watch yourself, Jacko. . . .

FOURTH SOLDIER. Just watch me do the 100 yards in . . .

He runs off – bullet gets him.

SERGEANT. Now if he's been shot, I'll kill him.

SECOND SOLDIER. He has, Serg.

SERGEANT. Well – I reckon we all better stick together.

Heavy gun.

They've started shelling for the next attack.

ALL. Who ?

SERGEANT. The bloody mad English. Come on, let's get the hell out of here.

SECOND SOLDIER. Where shall we go ?

SERGEANT. That's the question.

Heavy gun and explosion.

ALL (*shouting*). It's us. Stop shooting. It's us.

Bullet shot. They all turn and face downstage.

Kamerad – Kamerad . . .

'Ping' from the band. They freeze, then reel off as if in a dream.

SERGEANT. This is it.

Ping.

SECOND SOLDIER. Is it, Serg ?

THIRD SOLDIER. It's not so bad.

FIRST SOLDIER. No.

Ping.

SERGEANT. We've escaped the whole blooming war now.

SECOND SOLDIER. I'll see ya, Serg.

SERGEANT. See ya.

They go off.

The M.C. comes in and sets a stand for Mrs Pankhurst. During the following scene he wanders round the stage as a silent observer. Mrs Pankhurst and a crowd of bystanders come on. As she climbs on her box the crowd whistle.

FIRST MAN. Shut up!

MRS PANKHURST. Now, before talking to you all, I should like to read you a letter from my friend George Bernard Shaw.

SECOND MAN. Who's he when he's at home?

FIRST WOMAN. Ain't it disgusting?

MRS PANKHURST. He says: 'The men of this country are being sacrificed to the blunders of boobies, the cupidity of capitalists, the ambition of conquerors, the lusts and lies and rancours of bloodthirsts that love war, because it opens their prison doors and sets them on the throne of power and popularity.'

THIRD MAN. Now give us a song!

MRS PANKHURST. For the second time peace is being offered to the sorely tried people of the civilized world . . .

SECOND MAN. Hallo.

MRS PANKHURST. . . . at the close of 1915 President Wilson proposed an immediate armistice; to be followed by a peace conference . . .

SECOND MAN. 'Hallo!

MRS PANKHURST. . . . in April of this year, Germany herself proposed peace . . .

SECOND MAN. Hallo! Hallo!

MRS PANKHURST. . . . the peace movements are strong in England, France and the United States; and in Germany. In the Reichstag . . .

SECOND MAN. Who's he when he's at home?

MRS PANKHURST. . . . the peace groups are active and outspoken; the exact terms of Germany's offer have never been made known to us and I should like to ask Lloyd George what his war aims are.

FIRST WOMAN. I should like to ask you what your old man has for dinner!

MRS PANKHURST. . . . the politicians chatter like imbeciles while civilization bleeds to death.

THIRD MAN. You're talking like a traitor. Pacifists are traitors.

MRS PANKHURST. I ask that gentleman . . .

THIRD MAN. Don't ask me . . . 'Cos I don't know nothing . . . I'm stupid.

MRS PANKHURST. . . . to consider the plight of the civilized world after another year: you do not know what you do and the statesmen wash their hands of the whole affair . . .

FOURTH MAN. Why don't you wash your face!

SECOND MAN. Douglas Haig's got them on the run.

MRS PANKHURST. Who tells you this? *The Times* . . .

SECOND MAN. He's got them going.

MRS PANKHURST. . . . the newspaper that refuses to publish the pacifist letters, and distorts the facts of our so-called victories. We are killing off slowly but surely the best of the male population . . .

FIRST WOMAN. Here! Don't you address them words to me . . .

SECOND WOMAN. Here! Don't you address them words to her . . .

MRS PANKHURST. . . . the sons of Europe are being crucified . . .

FIRST WOMAN. . . . my old man's at the front . . .

SECOND WOMAN. She's had her share of suffering . . .

MRS PANKHURST. . . . on the barbed wire, because you . . .

FIRST WOMAN. Here, don't you address them words to me; my old man's at the front.

MRS PANKHURST. . . . you the misguided masses are crying out for it.

SECOND WOMAN. Her old man's at the front.

FIRST WOMAN. My old man's at the front.

MRS PANKHURST. War cannot be won. No one can win a war. Is it your wish this war will go on and on until Germany is beaten to the ground?

NEWSPANEL. JULY I . . . SOMME . . . BRITISH LOSS 60,000 MEN ON THE FIRST DAY.

CROWD. Yes! Yes!

They drown her with shouts. They sing.

SONG.   RULE, BRITANNIA

> Rule, Britannia, Britannia rules the waves,
> Britons, never, never, never shall be slaves.
> Rule, Britannia, Britannia rules the waves,
> Britons never, never, never shall . . .

Two drunken soldiers come on as the crowd goes off, and sing.

SONG.   I DON'T WANT TO BE A SOLDIER

(*Tune: 'I'll make a man of you'*)

> I don't want to be a soldier,
> I don't want to go to war,
> I'd rather stay at home,
> Around the streets to roam,
> And live on the earnings of a lady typist.
> I don't want a bayonet in my belly,
> I don't want my bollocks shot away,
> I'd rather stay in England,
> In merry, merry England,
> And fornicate my bleeding life away.

The other soldiers run on.

HAIG (*entering*). Attack on the Somme!

M.C. Right dress! Eyes front! Left turn! We're going along the line.

SERGEANT. Quick march!

The men march round the stage whistling 'Pop Goes the Weasel'. They end up kneeling in line behind Haig.

HAIG. We shall launch a decisive attack which will carry us through the German lines. We shall advance on Belgium to the Channel Ports. The people at home have given us the means to mass every man, horse, and gun on the Western

Front. It is our duty to attack the enemy until his last resources are exhausted and his line breaks. Then in will go our cavalry and annihilate him. I am the predestined instrument of providence for the achievement of victory for the British Army.

Two Englishwomen enter on either side of the stage and shout across to one another.

FIRST ENGLISHWOMAN. Hey, Bett!
SECOND ENGLISHWOMAN. Yeah? What?
FIRST ENGLISHWOMAN. You know what they're doing now?
SECOND ENGLISHWOMAN. No, what?
FIRST ENGLISHWOMAN. Melting corpses for glycerine.
SECOND ENGLISHWOMAN. Get away! Who?
FIRST ENGLISHWOMAN. The Germans. It's in this morning's paper.

Two German women enter on the balconies, left and right, and shout to one another.

FIRST GERMAN WOMAN. Emma! Emma!
SECOND GERMAN WOMAN. Ja?
FIRST GERMAN WOMAN. Weisst du, was sie jetzt tun?
SECOND GERMAN WOMAN. Nein, was?
FIRST GERMAN WOMAN. Sie schmelzen Körper für Glyzerin.
SECOND GERMAN WOMAN. Wirklich! Wer?
FIRST GERMAN WOMAN. Die Engländer. Es war in der Zeitung heute Morgen.
FIRST ENGLISHWOMAN. Bett – do you want to know something else? They say there's another big push coming.
SECOND ENGLISHWOMAN. Oh God.
FIRST GERMAN WOMAN (*during preceding two speeches*). Emma! Man sagt noch ein Angriff kommt.
SECOND GERMAN WOMAN. Sagst du? Mein Gott.

The four women go off.

HAIG. Advance!

The soldiers rise and march round singing.

SONG.   KAISER BILL

(*Tune: 'Pop goes the Weasel'*)

Kaiser Bill is feeling ill,
The Crown Prince, he's gone barmy.
We don't give a cluck for old von Fluck
And all his bleeding army.

AUSTRALIAN VOICE (*from auditorium*). Are you the reinforce-
ments?

SERGEANT. Yeah! On our way up to Vimy.

VOICE. Wouldn't go up there if I were you; they've got a
shortage!

ONE OF THE SOLDIERS. What of? Ammunition?

VOICE. No. Coffins!

SERGEANT. Right, lads. Form fours. Rum ration.

The men kneel again.

HAIG. It's now or never.

BRITISH GENERAL. Runners!

*The men are centre stage and sing, marking time. Two runners
set up tables with field telephones at opposite sides of the stage.
Haig and the British General sit talking into the phones and
two runners cross backwards and forwards taking messages.*

SONG.   THEY WERE ONLY PLAYING LEAPFROG

(*Tune: 'John Brown's Body'*)

One staff officer jumped right over another staff officer's
back.

And another staff officer jumped right over that other staff
officer's back,

A third staff officer jumped right over two other staff
officers' backs,

And a fourth staff officer jumped right over all the other
staff officers' backs.

They were only playing leapfrog,

They were only playing leapfrog,

They were only playing leapfrog,

When one staff officer jumped right over another staff
officer's back.

*The song is sung a second time quietly under Haig and the
British General, who are talking simultaneously.*

HAIG. Hello. G.O.C.-in-C. Clear the line, please. Look, I must
have the Eighth Division forward on the right . . . Yes I
must have Eighth Division . . . I see, seventy per cent
casualties . . . I must have Eighth Division forward on the
right wing . . . (*The following sentence heard clearly.*) No,
you must reserve the artillery; we are using too many shells.

BRITISH GENERAL. Are you ready there? We are ready here
. . . Have receipted your orders to advance . . . Are you
ready there? . . . We are ready here . . . Are you ready
there? . . . We are ready here . . . and approved. . . .
(*The following sentence heard clearly.*) Night has fallen. The
clouds are gathering. The men are lost somewhere in no-
man's-land.

RUNNER. Seventy per cent casualties, sir.

BRITISH GENERAL. Then there is a corner of some foreign land
that is forever England.

HAIG. We shall attack at dawn!

SERGEANT. Right. Dig in for the night, lads. Packs off.

*Haig and the British General continue working at their tables.
The soldiers remove their kit and settle down for the night.*

FIRST SOLDIER (*sings*). Old soldiers never die,

The young ones wish they would.

SECOND SOLDIER. Can you hear those poor wounded bleeders
moaning in no-man's-land?

THIRD SOLDIER. Sounds like a cattle market.
HAIG. Attack at five ack emma.
BRITISH GENERAL. Attack, five ack emma.

The two runners sleep, standing up. The soldiers sing softly.

SONG.   IF YOU WANT THE OLD BATTALION

> If you want the old battalion,
> We know where they are, we know where they are,
> We know where they are,
> If you want the old battalion, we know where they are,
> They're hanging on the old barbed wire,
> We've seen them, we've seen them,
> Hanging on the old barbed wire,
> We've seen them, we've seen them,
> Hanging on the old barbed wire.

HAIG. Monday, noon. Our offensive commenced this morning; satisfactory progress. Monday evening. The trouble was
   that the men waved their hats instead of flags as His Majesty
   rode by. I tried the mare out the day before. The King did
   clutch the reins too firmly . . . correction . . . the King
   did clutch the reins rather firmly. No reflection on His
   Majesty's horsemanship. The grass was very slippery and
   the mare moved backwards; she was upset. I'd exercised her
   every day for a year.

SONG.   FAR FAR FROM WIPERS (*Tune: 'Sing me to sleep'*)

> Far far from Wipers, I long to be,
> Where German snipers can't get at me,
> Damp is my dugout, cold are my feet,
> Waiting for whizzbangs to put me to sleep.

A bugle sounds reveille.

HAIG. So unfortunate it had to be my horse that threw the
   King.

Reveille sounds again.

HAIG'S RUNNER. Five ack emma, sir.

HAIG (*into the telephone*). Press the attack immediately.

BRITISH GENERAL (*into the telephone*). The losses were very heavy last night, sir. The Canadian corps had very heavy casualties . . .

He continues his report on losses. The soldiers begin to pick up their kit. One of them sings.

SONG.   IF THE SERGEANT STEALS YOUR RUM

(*Tune: 'Never Mind'*)

If the sergeant steals your rum, never mind,
If the sergeant steals your rum, never mind;
Though he's just a blinking sot,
Let him have the bloody lot,
If the sergeant steals your rum, never mind.

BRITISH GENERAL (*continuing*). . . . the 13th London were isolated and completely wiped out by their own cross-fire.

HAIG. There must be no squeamishness over losses. Give orders to advance immediately.

The two officers retire upstage and watch.

SERGEANT. Right, over the top, boys.

Explosion. They charge and fling themselves on the ground. Machine-guns.

Jerry's doin' well.

FIRST SOLDIER. What are all them little yellow flags out there?

SECOND SOLDIER. They give them to our blokes.

FIRST SOLDIER. What for?

SECOND SOLDIER. So they'd know where we was.

SERGEANT. Did you say our blokes?

SECOND SOLDIER. Yea.

FIRST SOLDIER. Oh, I get it, so our guns don't get us before Jerry does.

Explosion.

SERGEANT. You stick with me, lads. I'll see you through this lot. Heads down and keep spread well out.

SECOND SOLDIER (*sings*). Far far from Wipers I long to be.

SERGEANT. Blimey! You still here?

SECOND SOLDIER. Yeah! Why?

SERGEANT. I drew you in the sweep.

A shell explodes.

I've had enough of this.

SECOND SOLDIER. Me and all.

SERGEANT. Every man for himself.

THIRD SOLDIER. Every man for himself.

SECOND SOLDIER. See you after the war, sarg.

SERGEANT. Yeah, in the Red Lion.

FIRST SOLDIER. Eight o'clock.

SERGEANT. Make it half past.

FIRST SOLDIER. Eh?

SERGEANT. I might be a bit late.

The soldiers go off.

BRITISH GENERAL. Permission to speak, sir? I have been wondering, or rather the staff and I have been wondering, perhaps this policy of attrition might be a mistake. After all, it's wearing us down more than it is them. Couldn't we try a policy of manoeuvre on other fronts?

HAIG. Nonsense. The Western Front is the only real front. We must grind them down. You see, our population is greater than theirs and their losses are greater than ours.

BRITISH GENERAL. I don't quite follow that, sir.

HAIG. In the end they will have five thousand men left and we will have ten thousand and we shall have won. In any case, I

I wore a tunic, a dirty khaki tunic,
And you wore your civvy clothes . . .

intend to launch one more full-scale offensive, and we shall break through and win.

JUNIOR OFFICER (*entering*). I say, sir, did you know that the average life of a young subaltern at the front has now increased to three weeks.

SECOND OFFICER (*entering*). Yes, sir, and replacements are coming in by the thousand; it's marvellous. (*Exit.*)

JUNIOR OFFICER. It's an empire in arms. (*Exit.*)

HAIG. You see, the staff are in complete accord.

BRITISH GENERAL. Yes, sir. And the morale of the civilian population has never been higher.

The murderer, Landru, enters, dragging the body of a woman followed by a gendarme.

LANDRU. Excusez-moi, s'il vous plaît.

GENDARME. Hey! M. Landru! Where are you going with that body?

LANDRU. I am going to bury it. With all this killing going on and they never called me up, I thought I'd settle a few private scores.

GENDARME. Good idea! . . . How many have you done?

LANDRU. Twelve wives, so far.

GENDARME. Hey! Just a minute. You're for the guillotine.

Both go off.

NEWSPANEL. NOVEMBER . . . SOMME BATTLE ENDS . .
  TOTAL LOSS 1,332,000 MEN . . . GAIN NIL.

The band plays a few bars of 'Twelfth Street Rag'. Three couples dance wildly and continue as the soldier in uniform sings.

SONG.   I WORE A TUNIC
                (*Tune: 'I wore a Tulip'*)

I wore a tunic, a dirty khaki tunic,
And you wore your civvy clothes,

We fought and bled at Loos, while you were on the booze,
The booze that no one here knows.
You were out with the wenches, while we were in the
    trenches,
Facing an angry foe,
Oh, you were a-slacking, while we were attacking
The Germans on the Menin Road.

*The dancers go off. Haig, a chaplain, a nurse and soldiers
come on.*

CHAPLAIN. Let us pray.

*All sing. The soldiers sing their own version of the hymns. The
chaplain, Haig, and the nurse sing the correct words.*

SONG.   FORWARD JOE SOAP'S ARMY

(*Tune: 'Onward Christian Soldiers'*)

Forward Joe Soap's army, marching without fear,
With our old commander, safely in the rear.
He boasts and skites from morn till night,
And thinks he's very brave,
But the men who really did the job are dead and in their
    grave.
Forward Joe Soap's army, marching without fear,
With our old commander, safely in the rear.
Amen.

CHAPLAIN. Dearly beloved brethren, I am sure you will be
    glad to hear the news from the Home Front. The Arch-
    bishop of Canterbury has made it known that it is no sin to
    labour for the war on the Sabbath. I am sure you would like
    to know that the Chief Rabbi has absolved your Jewish
    brethren from abstaining from pork in the trenches. And
    likewise his Holiness the Pope has ruled that the eating of
    flesh on a Friday is no longer a venial sin . . .
SOLDIER. High time we had an Irish pope . . .

SECOND SOLDIER. You're right.

CHAPLAIN. And in far-away Tibet, the Dalai Llama has placed his prayers at the disposal of the Allies. Now, brethren, tomorrow being Good Friday, we hope God will look kindly on our attack on Arras.

MEN. Amen.

SERGEANT. We will now sing from Hymns Ancient and Modern, number 358, 'Waft, Waft, ye winds, waft, waft ye'.

SONG.   FRED KARNO'S ARMY

(Tune: 'The Church's One Foundation')

We are Fred Karno's army,
The Ragtime Infantry,
We cannot fight, we cannot shoot,
What bleeding use are we?
And when we get to Berlin,
The Kaiser he will say,
Hoch, hoch, mein Gott, what a bloody rotten lot,
Are the Ragtime infantry!
Amen.

CHAPLAIN. Let us pray. O God, show thy face to us as thou didst with thy angel at Mons. The choir will now sing 'What a friend we have in Jesus' as we offer a silent prayer for Sir Douglas Haig for success in tomorrow's onset.

SONG.   WHEN THIS LOUSY WAR IS OVER

(Tune: 'What a friend we have in Jesus')

When this lousy war is over,
No more soldiering for me,
When I get my civvy clothes on,
Oh, how happy I shall be!
No more church parades on Sunday,
No more putting in for leave,

> I shall kiss the sergeant-major,
> How I'll miss him, how he'll grieve!
> Amen.

CHAPLAIN. O Lord, now lettest thou thy servant depart in peace, according to thy word. Dismiss.

CORPORAL (*blowing a whistle*). Come on, you men, fall in.

The soldiers sing as they march off.

SONG.   WASH ME IN THE WATER

> Whiter than the whitewash on the wall,
> Whiter than the whitewash on the wall,
> Oh, wash me in the water that you wash your dirty daughter in,
> And I shall be whiter than the whitewash on the wall,
> On the wall . . .

CHAPLAIN. Land of our birth, we pledge to thee, our love and toil in the years to be.

HAIG. Well, God, the prospects for a successful attack are now ideal. I place myself in thy hands.

CHAPLAIN. Into thy hands I commend my spirit.

NURSE. The fields are full of tents, O Lord, all empty except for as yet unmade and naked iron bedsteads. Every ward has been cleared to make way for the wounded that will be arriving when the big push comes.

HAIG. I trust you will understand, Lord, that as a British gentleman I could not subordinate myself to the ambitions of a junior foreign commander, as the politicians suggested. It is for the prestige of my King and Empire, Lord.

CHAPLAIN. Teach us to rule ourself alway, controlled and cleanly night and day.

HAIG. I ask thee for victory, Lord, before the Americans arrive.

NURSE. The doctors say there will be enormous numbers of dead and wounded, God.

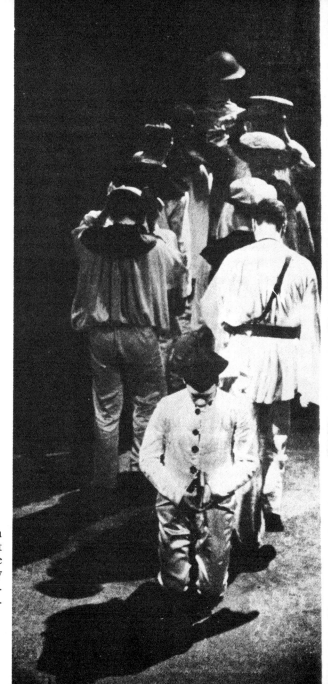

Oh Lord
ow lettest thou
thy servant
depart in peace
ccording to thy
word.
Dismiss.

CHAPLAIN. That we may bring if need arise, no maimed or worthless sacrifice.

HAIG. Thus to grant us fair weather for tomorrow's attack, that we may drive the enemy into the sea.

NURSE. O Lord, I beg you, do not let this dreadful war cause all the suffering that we have prepared for. I know you will answer my prayer.

Explosion. They go off.

A sequence of slides is shown as soldiers' voices sing offstage.

Slide 42: A group of eight or nine Highland infantrymen, around a small camp fire.

Slide 43: Two captured wounded German infantrymen, both sitting, one nursing a badly wounded leg, the other sewing.

Slide 44: A lull in the fighting. A trench of Tommies 'at ease' – some smoking, others doing running repairs on their kit.

Slide 45: Three Tommies walking through a rain-soaked muddy field.

Slide 46: Two captured Germans between two Tommies. One of the Germans is being given a drink of water by one of the Tommies.

Slide 47: A group of Tommies, skylarking and obviously off-duty, with a damaged old horse-drawn coach, upon which they've chalked '10 Downing Street'.

SONG.   I WANT TO GO HOME

> [42] I want to go home, [43] I want to go home, [44]
> I don't want to go in the trenches no more,
> Where whizzbangs and shrapnel they whistle and roar.
> [45]
> Take me over the sea, [46] where the alleyman can't get at
> me; [47]
> Oh my, I don't want to die, I want to go home.

NEWSPANEL: BY NOV 1916 . . . TWO AND A HALF MILLION MEN KILLED ON WESTERN FRONT.

The screen goes up to reveal soldiers in gas capes doing burial squad duty in mime. Haig is on one of the balconies.

HAIG. I thank you, God; the attack is a great success. Fighting has been severe, but that was to be expected. There has been some delay along the Menin Road, but the ground is thick with enemy dead. First reports from the clearing station state that our casualties are only some sixty thousand: mostly slight. The wounded are very cheery indeed.

The soldiers sing as they work.

SONG.   THE BELLS OF HELL

> The bells of hell go ting-a-ling-a-ling,
> For you but not for me,
> And the little devils how they sing-a-ling-a-ling,
> For you but not for me.
> Oh death, where is thy sting-a-ling-a-ling,
> Oh grave, thy victory?
> The bells of hell go ting-a-ling-a-ling
> For you but not for me.

NEWSPANEL. APRIL 17 . . . AISNE . . . ALLIED LOSS 180,000 MEN . . . GAIN NIL.

The soldiers sing again, more gaily. Haig conducts them, wearing a pierrot hat, as they dance.

> The bells of hell go ting-a-ling-a-ling,
> For you but not for me,
> And the little devils how they sing-a-ling-a-ling
> For you but not for me.
> O death, where is thy sting-a-ling-a-ling
> Oh grave, thy victory?
> The bells of hell go ting-a-ling-a-ling
> For you but not for me.

A medical officer and a nurse enter.

MEDICAL OFFICER. We'll have to start burning them soon, nurse.

NURSE. Yes, it's such an unpleasant duty, doctor. The men always try to get out of it.

MEDICAL OFFICER. Oh, well, it'll be good farming country after.

NURSE. If there are any of us left to see it.

FIRST SOLDIER. Still got my water on the knee, doc.

MEDICAL OFFICER. I'll fix you up with a number nine later.

FIRST SOLDIER. On my knee! – I said, sir!

SERGEANT. All right, you men. I want this trench clear in half an hour; get stuck in. Come on, jump to it!

The men form up, as in a slit trench, digging.

BAND.   OH IT'S A LOVELY WAR
                    (*Very slow*)

HAIG (*reading a letter*). From Snowball to Douglas. Water and mud are increasing and becoming horrible. The longer days when they come will be most welcome, especially to the officers, who say the conditions are impairing their efficiency. The other ranks don't seem to mind so much.

FIRST SOLDIER. Look out – we're awash! Hey, give us a hand; he's going under.

SECOND SOLDIER. Cor – he's worse than old Fred.

THIRD SOLDIER. Here, whatever happened to old Fred?

SECOND SOLDIER. I dunno. Haven't seen him since his last cry for help.

FOURTH SOLDIER. That's right; he got sucked under.

THIRD SOLDIER. Oh no, he went sick.

FIFTH SOLDIER. No, he went under.

THIRD SOLDIER. He went sick.

SECOND SOLDIER. He got sucked under, mate.

THIRD SOLDIER. Well, I bet you a fag he went sick.

SECOND SOLDIER. Don't be daft. You can't go sick here. You've got to lose your lungs, your liver, your lights . . .

SERGEANT. Watch it!

The Nurse crossing in front stumbles.

FIRST SOLDIER. I think she's lost hers.
NURSE. Thank you.
MEDICAL OFFICER. Put that man on a charge, sergeant.
FIRST SOLDIER. On a raft.
HAIG. Everything points to a complete breakdown in enemy morale. Now is the time to hit him resolutely and firmly. I understand the Prime Minister has been asking questions about my strategy. I cannot believe a British Minister could be so ungentlemanly.

The soldiers go off.

NURSE (*writing*). Thank you for the copy of *The Times*. I am glad that in spite of all it is still a victory; it does not seem so here. It is beyond belief, the butchery; the men look so appalling when they are brought in and so many die.
HAIG. September 17th. Glass still falling. A light breeze blew from the south. Weather unsettled.

NEWSPANEL. AVERAGE LIFE OF A MACHINE GUNNER UNDER ATTACK . . . FOUR MINUTES

The Nurse sings.

SONG.   KEEP THE HOME FIRES BURNING

They were summoned from the hillside,
They were called in from the glen,
And the country found them ready
At the stirring call for men.
Let no tears add to their hardship,
As the soldiers pass along,
And although your heart is breaking,
Make it sing this cheery song:

Keep the Home Fires burning
While your hearts are yearning,
Though the lads are far away,
They dream of home.
There's a silver lining,
Through the dark clouds shining,
Turn the dark cloud inside out,
Till the boys come home.

Four girls enter.

FIRST GIRL. Oh, look, it's another casualty list. Makes you shiver.

NEWSPANEL. SEPT 20 . . . MENIN ROAD . . . BRITISH LOSS 22,000 MEN GAIN 800 YARDS . . . SEPT 25 . . . POLYGON WOOD . . . BRITISH LOSS 17,000 MEN GAIN 1,000 YARDS.

SECOND GIRL. Who's on it?

THIRD GIRL. Ee, all those Arkwrights.

FIRST GIRL. That's three she's lost.

SECOND GIRL. No, that's four she's lost.

FIRST GIRL. No, three.

THIRD GIRL. That'll be Harry Arkwright, who used to work at the mill.

FOURTH GIRL. Hey, what are you looking at?

SECOND GIRL. Casualty list.

FOURTH GIRL. Oh, my God – let me have a look.

THIRD GIRL. Oh, look, all those Arkwrights; they're bringing them home at night now.

SECOND GIRL. They're letting them out of the prisons and all.

FOURTH GIRL. What for?

SECOND GIRL. 'Cos they say there's another big push coming.

FOURTH GIRL. Oh, I know that. I work in the munitions factory. We're the first to know about these things, of course.

FIRST GIRL. Get a good screw, don't you?

FOURTH GIRL. Oh, my God, yes. Do you know, one girl in my department earned three pound last week.

FIRST GIRL. Go on.

FOURTH GIRL. That's where the money is.

SECOND GIRL. I wouldn't like to work down there. All those men.

FOURTH GIRL. Yes, it is a bit dangerous at times. We had an explosion last week and one of the women got blown to smithereens. It's no use worrying, though – you've got to carry on.

FIRST GIRL. We're on overtime, you know.

FOURTH GIRL. Of course, you're in cotton, aren't you?

FIRST GIRL. That's right and we're on some funny stuff at the moment – they say it's for shrouds. Oh, it makes you shiver.

FOURTH GIRL. Oh, my God, enough to give you the willies; I'd rather be in munitions. Oh, what's that there?

BAND.   WALTZING MATILDA

SECOND GIRL. 'Ere, what's that, then?

FOURTH GIRL. Eh! It's a brass band.

FIRST GIRL. Hey, it's the Aussies!

FOURTH GIRL. Up the Anzacs!

NEWSPANEL. OCT 12 . . . PASSCHENDAELE . . . BRIT-ISH LOSS 13,000 MEN IN 3 HOURS . . . GAIN 100 YARDS.

FIRST GIRL. Lovely and brown, aren't they?

THIRD GIRL. They're a handsome lot.

FOURTH GIRL. Lovely fellows.

FIRST GIRL. Oh, they've gone.

FOURTH GIRL. Eh! I forgot. My sister's down at your place in cotton.

FIRST GIRL. What, in shrouds?

FOURTH GIRL. No, shirts.

She sings. The other girls go off.

SONG.   SISTER SUSIE'S SEWING SHIRTS

Yes. Sister Susie's sewing shirts for soldiers,
Such skill at sewing shirts my shy young sister Susie
shows,
Some soldiers send epistles, say they'd sooner sleep on
thistles,
Than the saucy, soft, short shirts for soldiers, sister Susie
sews.

FOURTH GIRL. Hey, the war won't go on for ever. Let's have a
sing-song, shall we. If I sing it again, will you join in with
me ? Go on, don't look so gloomy.

She sings.

Sister Susie's sewing shirts for soldiers,
Such skill at sewing shirts my shy young sister Susie
shows,
Some soldiers send epistles, say they'd sooner sleep on
thistles,
Than the saucy, soft, short shirts for soldiers, sister Susie
sews.
Come on.

*She sings the chorus at double speed, but doesn't sing the last
line, saying to the audience:*

I can't hear you – can you sing up ?

Meanwhile two pierrots come on with three hats.

NEWSPANEL. 800,000 GERMANS STARVE TO DEATH
THROUGH BRITISH BLOCKADE.

FIRST PIERROT (*wearing British General's hat*). The prospects
for 1918 are excellent. This year will see final victory.
FOURTH GIRL (*to audience*). Oh, here's Mutt and Jeff again.

SECOND PIERROT (*wearing German helmet*). Sieg für Deutschland.

FIRST PIERROT (*putting on French kèpi*). Et pour la France la gloire et la victoire.

SECOND PIERROT (*wearing German helmet*). Gott mit uns. (*Puts on British General's hat.*) And with us, old boy. If we continue this campaign the way we are going, we'll sew the entire thing up by 1918.

FIRST PIERROT (*putting on German helmet*). Neunzehn hundert, neunzehn.

SECOND PIERROT. Nineteen twenty, twenty-five.

FIRST PIERROT. Fünf und zwanzig, dreizig . . .

SECOND PIERROT. Thirty, thirty-five . . . forty: forty-five, fifty, fifty-five, sixty, sixty-three, sixty-four – any advance on sixty-four ? Plenty more numbers where they came from.

THE PIERROTS AND THE GIRLS. Some soldiers send epistles, say they'd sooner sleep on thistles,

Than the saucy, soft, short shirts for soldiers,

Sister Susie sews.

Exeunt.

BAND.   MARSEILLAISE

French soldiers line up for an advance.

FRENCH OFFICER. Alors. Again for the glory of France, prepare for the attack. En avant! . . . En avant! . . . Are you deaf?

FRENCH SOLDIER. Non, mon Capitaine.

FRENCH OFFICER. What is this ? A mutiny ?

FRENCH SOLDIER. We think it is stupid to go into the trenches again.

FRENCH OFFICER. You don't think – you obey. If you refuse, you will be shot!

FRENCH SOLDIER. Very well. We follow you – like lambs to the slaughter.

FRENCH OFFICER. Bon. Like lambs to the slaughter . . . Pour la gloire de la France! En avant!

FRENCH SOLDIER. Baaa.
FRENCH OFFICER. Vive la République!

The men begin to advance towards the footlights.

SOLDIERS. Baaa.
FRENCH OFFICER. En avant!
SOLDIERS. Baaa – baa.
FRENCH OFFICER AND SOLDIERS. Baaa – baaa – baaa . . .

There is a burst of machine-gun fire. They collapse. Pause.

FRENCH SOLDIER. Adieu la vie.

All sing.

SONG.   CHANSON DE CRAONNE

Adieu la vie,
Adieu l'amour,
Adieu à toutes les femmes.
C'est bien fini,
C'est pour toujours,
De cette guerre infâme.
C'est à Craonne,
Sur le plateau,
Qu'ils ont laissé leur peau:
Car ils sont tous condamnés,
Ce sont les sacrifiés.

SONG.   I DON'T WANT TO BE A SOLDIER

I don't want to be a soldier,
I don't want to go to war,
I'd rather stay at home,
Around the streets to roam,
And live off the earnings of a lady typist.

NEWSPANEL. THE WAR TO END WARS . . . KILLED TEN
MILLION . . . WOUNDED TWENTY-ONE MILLION . . .
. . . . MISSING SEVEN MILLION.

I don't want a bayonet in my belly,
I don't want my bollocks shot away,
I'd rather stay in England,
In merry, merry England,
And fornicate my bleeding life away.

Slide Sequence:

Slide 42: Repeated.

Slide 48: Canadian infantrymen in trench. One fast asleep, another writing home.

Slide 31: Repeated.

Slide 49: Five Tommies trying to pull a field gun out of the mud.

Slide 50: A company of French Poilus marching past with rifles at the slope.

Slide 51: Two weary British officers, both in battle dress, one with bandaged head.

Slide 52: Two young Canadian soldiers, leaning against spiked boards, one writing a letter.

Slide 53: A long line of Tommies walking away from the camera, following the direction of a trench.

SONG.   AND WHEN THEY ASK US

(*Tune: 'They wouldn't believe me'*)

[42] And when they ask us, how dangerous it was, [48]
Oh, we'll never tell them, no, we'll never tell them: [31]
We spent our pay in some café, [49]
And fought wild women night and day,
'Twas the cushiest job we ever had. [50]

And when they ask us, and they're certainly going to ask us, [51]
The reason why we didn't win the Croix de Guerre, [52]
Oh, we'll never tell them, oh, we'll never tell them [53]
There was a front, but damned if we knew where.

And when they ask us, and they're certainly going to ask us,
The reason why we didn't win the Croix de Guerre,
Oh, we'll never tell them, oh, we'll never tell them
There was a front, but damned if we knew where!

FINALE.   OH IT'S A LOVELY WAR

Oh, oh, oh, it's a lovely war,
What do we want with eggs and ham,
When we've got plum and apple jam?
Form fours, right turn,
How shall we spend the money we earn?
Oh, oh, oh, it's a lovely,
Oh, oh, oh, it's a lovely,
Oh, oh, oh, it's a lovely war!

CURTAIN

APPENDIX

Source material for '*OH WHAT A LOVELY WAR*'

'*The Times*' *History of the War*
'*I Was There*', published weekly about 1934, later assembled
   into three volumes and published by Amalgamated Press
The First World War, Colonel Repington (2 volumes)
My War Memories, General Ludendorff (2 volumes)
Earl Haig, Brigadier-General Charteris
Haig, Duff Cooper
Haig's Diaries
Field-Marshal Wilson, Sir C. E. Callwell
War Memoirs, Lloyd George
How We Lived Then – 1914–1918, Mrs C. S. Peel
C.Q.G., Jean Pierrefeu
Mutiny 1917, John Williams
Memoirs of an Infantry Officer, Siegfried Sassoon
Undertones of War, Edmund Blunden
In Flanders Fields, Leon Wolff
Mr Punch's History of the War
A History of the World War, Liddell Hart
The First World War, Cyril Falls
Memoirs, Franz von Papen
Diplomatic Documents, H.M.S.O., 1915
1914, F. M. French
The March on Paris, 1914, General von Cluck
The First Hundred Thousand, Ian Hay
Regimental Histories
The Great War, H. W. Wilson (13 volumes)
August 1914, B. Tuchman
Brass Hat: The Story of General Wilson
The Donkeys, Alan Clark

The Illustrated War News (published weekly during the war)

Contemporary newspapers (in the possession of G. Sewell)

European History 1815–1918, C. J. Pennithorne Hughes

Pageant of the Century, Odhams Press, published 1935

Covenants with Death, Express Newspapers

The First World War, Illustrated Express Newspapers

World War, published weekly about 1937

Twenty Years After, published weekly 1937

The Great War (The World Crisis), Winston Churchill

A Soldier's Diary, Ralph Scott

Memoirs of a Foxhunting Man, Siegfried Sassoon

Goodbye to all That, Robert Graves

The '*Phillip Maddison*' series of novels by Henry Williamson

Mons, John Terraine

Official History of the War

Die Blutige International, Kirsch

Works of Phillip Noel-Baker

Merchants of Death, Engelbrecht and Heiniger

Works of Herman Kahn

Verdun, Jules Romains

Covenant with Death, John Harris

The Sphere, Illustrated London News

Writings of Philip Gibbs

Records of: *The Times, Daily Express, Daily Mail, Evening Standard*

Charles Chilton's notes and songs, and many other publications of which no note has been kept.

Methuen's Modern Plays

Bertolt Brecht *Mother Courage*
The Caucasian Chalk Circle
The Good Person of Szechwan
The Life of Galileo
Syd Cheatle *Straight Up*
Shelagh Delaney *A Taste of Honey*
The Lion in Love
Max Frisch *The Fire Raisers*
Andorra
Jean Giraudoux *Tiger at the Gates*
Peter Handke *O Hending the Audience* and
Self - Accusation
Rolf Hochhuth *The Representative*
Heinar Kipphardt *In the Matter of J. Robert Oppenheimer*
Arthur Kopit *Chamber Music and other plays*
Indians
Jakov Lind *The Silver Foxes are Dead and other*
plays
David Mercer *On the Eve of Publication and other*
plays
After Haggerty
Flint
John Mortimer *The Judge*
Five Plays
Come As You Are
Joe Orton *Crimes of Passion*
Loot
What the Butler Saw
Funeral Games and *The Good and*
Faithful Servant

Harold Pinter	*The Birthday Party*
	The Room and *The Dumb Waiter*
	The Caretaker
	A Slight Ache and other plays
	The Collection and *The Lover*
	The Homecoming
	Tea Party and other plays
	Landscape and Silence
David Selbourne	*The Damned*
Jean-Paul Sartre	*Crime Passionnel*
Boris Vian	*The Empire Builders*
Theatre Workshop and Charles Chilton	*Oh What A Lovely War*
Charles Wood	*'H'*

*　　*　　*

Methuen's Theatre Classics

THE TROJAN WOMEN	Euripides
	an English version by Neil Curry
THE REDEMPTION	*adapted by Gordon Honeycombe from five cycles of Mystery Plays*
THE MISANTHROPE	Molière
	translated by Richard Wilbur
LADY PRECIOUS STREAM	*adapted by S. I. Hsiung from a sequence of traditional Chinese plays*
IRONHAND	Goethe
	adapted by John Arden
THE GOVERNMENT INSPECTOR	Gogol
	an English version by Edward O. Marsh and Jeremy Brooks

DANTON'S DEATH	Buechner *an English version by* *James Maxwell*
LONDON ASSURANCE	Boucicault *adapted and edited by* *Ronald Eyre*
BRAND	Ibsen
HEDDA GABLER	*translated by Michael Meyer*
THE WILD DUCK	
THE MASTER BUILDER	
MISS JULIE	Strindberg *translated by Michael Meyer*
THE IMPORTANCE OF BEING EARNEST	Wilde
LADY WINDERMERE'S FAN	
THE UBU PLAYS	Jarry *translated by Cyril Connolly* *and Simon Watson Taylor*
THE PLAYBOY OF THE WESTERN WORLD	Synge

★　　★　　★

Methuen Playscripts

Paul Ableman	*Tests*
	Blue Comedy
Barry Bermange	*Nathan and Tabileth* and *Oldenberg*
John Bowen	*The Corsican Brothers*
Howard Brenton	*Revenge*
	Christie in Love and other plays
Henry Chapman	*You won't always be on top*
Peter Cheeseman (Ed.)	*The Knotty*